Ireland

Ireland

BY JEAN F. BLASHFIELD

Enchantment of the World
Second Series

Children's Press®

A Division of Scholastic Inc.

NEW YORK   TORONTO   LONDON   AUCKLAND   SYDNEY
MEXICO CITY   NEW DELHI   HONG KONG
DANBURY, CONNECTICUT

Frontispiece: An Irishman with his donkey cart

Consultant: Dr. Patrick P. O'Neill, professor of English literature, University of
North Carolina, Chapel Hill

Please note: All statistics are as up-to-date as possible at the time of publication.

Book production by Herman Adler Design

Library of Congress Cataloging-in-Publication Data

Blashfield, Jean F.
    Ireland / by Jean F. Blashfield
        p. cm. — (Enchantment of the world. Second series)
    Includes bibliographical references and index.
    ISBN 0-516-21127-7
    1. Ireland—Juvenile literature. [1. Ireland.] I. Title. II. Series.
DA906 .B58 2002
941.5—dc21   00-066037

Acknowledgments

With grateful thanks to John Keenan of Navan, a man who knows a great deal about Ireland and loves to share the details. He provided the charm and the fun. The more nitty-gritty information on the Republic of Ireland and Northern Ireland was checked out in the excellent reference collections of the University of Wisconsin—Madison, UW—Whitewater, and Hedburg Public Library in Janesville, Wisconsin.

Cover photo:
Dunguaire Castle

Contents

Irish woolens for sale

Traditional Irish step dance

C H A P T E R

O N E

A Hundred Thousand Welcomes

8

It's been said that everybody is a little bit Irish. All of us delight in the charm of the Irish people. We grew up on Irish folktales about fairies and leprechauns. We feel comfortable when we visit, almost as if we'd been there before. And the Irish are glad we are. They are serious about the slogan used by their tourist trade: *Cead Mile Fáilte*—"A hundred thousand welcomes."

The world hasn't always looked so kindly upon the Irish. During the nineteenth century, many Irish people were forced to leave Ireland because of a serious crop failure and the fact that there were no jobs available. Huge numbers of them went to the United States and Canada. In the cities of those countries, advertisements for jobs often said, "No Irish need apply."

The island of Ireland was under British rule from 1169 to 1921. The Irish language was outlawed. The native culture was driven underground. Yet the Irish people never lost their Irishness or their yearning to be their own masters. Today, the people of the Republic of Ireland have finally achieved their dream.

Opposite: **A thatched-roof cottage**

This girl's smile captures the friendly spirit of the Irish people.

Geopolitical map
of Ireland

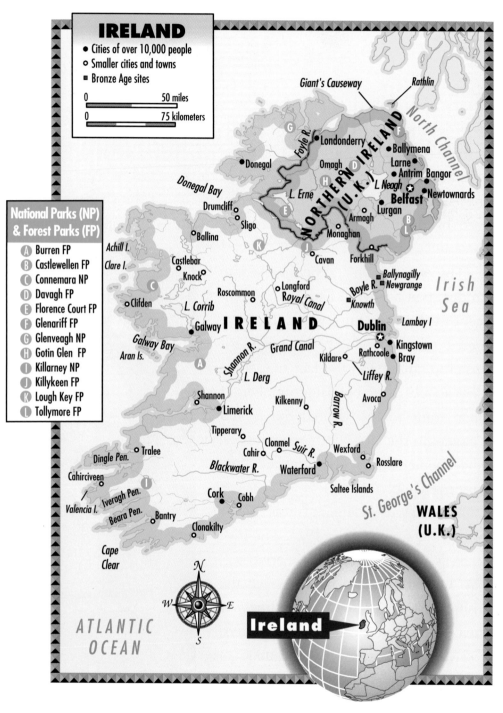

IRELAND

- Cities of over 10,000 people
- Smaller cities and towns
- Bronze Age sites

0 ————— 50 miles

0 ————— 75 kilometers

National Parks (NP) & Forest Parks (FP)

A Burren FP
B Castlewellen FP
C Connemara NP
D Davagh FP
E Florence Court FP
F Glenariff FP
G Glenveagh NP
H Gotin Glen FP
I Killarney NP
J Killykeen FP
K Lough Key FP
L Tollymore FP

Giant's Causeway   Rathlin

Foyle R.   G   Londonderry   F   North Channel
Donegal   Omagh   D   Ballymena
Donegal Bay   H   Larne   Bangor
Drumcliff   L. Erne   L Neagh   Antrim
E   Armagh   Belfast   Newtownards
Sligo   Lurgan
Ballina   Monaghan   B
Achill I.   K   Cavan   Forkhill
Clare I.   Castlebar   J   Ballynagilly
Knock   Longford   Boyle R.   Newgrange   Irish Sea
Roscommon   Royal Canal   Knowth
C   Clifden   L. Corrib   **IRELAND**   Lambay I
Galway   Dublin
Galway Bay   Grand Canal   Kingstown   Bray
Aran Is.   A   Shannon R.   Kildare   Rathcoole
L. Derg   Liffey R.
Shannon   Kilkenny   Barrow R.   Avoca
Limerick
Tipperary   Clonmel   Suir R.   Wexford
Cahir   Rosslare
Tralee   Blackwater R.   Waterford
Dingle Pen.   Saltee Islands   St. George's Channel
Cahirciveen   I   Cork   Cobh
Iveragh Pen.
Valencia I.   Beara Pen.   Bantry
Clonakilty   **WALES (U.K.)**
Cape Clear

NORTHERN IRELAND (U.K.)

ATLANTIC OCEAN

N
W   E
S

Ireland

10 *Ireland*

When a person is called Irish, he or she might be either from the Republic of Ireland or Northern Ireland—the northeastern part of the island that has been a province of the United Kingdom since 1921. It might seem as if all Irish people share the same heritage. However, many of the people in the northern part of the island are descended from Scottish Protestants who crossed the North Channel to live in Ireland two hundred years ago. The larger part of the island has a Catholic heritage.

Only in the twentieth century did the two parts of the island split into separate countries. It is a split that most Irish people still hope can somehow be repaired.

The Emerald Isle

Ireland is known for the many shades of green in its landscapes. Some people say there are forty. Others have identified hundreds. The name "Emerald Isle" has been used for green Ireland since the late eighteenth century, when it was coined by poet William Drennan.

The River Liffey

Ireland is known for its mystical beauty—there's enchantment in the mists lying in green valleys. Robust trees that bend dramatically in the wind off the ocean may be the home of the fairies, invisible creatures whom it isn't wise to anger. The rocks of ancient castles

What's in a Name?

In this book, the name "Ireland" will refer to the entire island up until 1921, when it was divided, or partitioned, into what became the Irish Free State (and then the Republic of Ireland) and Northern Ireland. After 1921, "Ireland" will refer to the Republic of Ireland, unless the subject is geography.

Other words that are important to know include:

Celtic. Refers to the Celts, people who spread throughout Europe in the centuries before the Common Era. Their culture remained in Ireland longer than anywhere else. The term also refers to the languages these people spoke.

Gaelic. The Celtic languages of Ireland, Scotland, and the Isle of Man (located between Ireland and England). Today, the Scottish language is most often called Scots Gaelic, or just Gaelic, while the Irish language is called Irish or Irish Gaelic. "Gaelic" also often refers to traditional cultural items or times of Ireland.

Éire. The official Irish-language name for the Republic of Ireland.

Hibernia. An old name for Ireland, used by the ancient Romans.

Irish. Describes any person from the entire island of Ireland or, more specifically, from the Republic of Ireland. Also, the Gaelic language still spoken in Ireland is called Irish.

Northern Irish. Describes any person, object, policy, or characteristic from Northern Ireland; often also means "Protestant," since the largest part of the population in Northern Ireland is Protestant.

Orangemen. Protestants from Northern Ireland, named after the Protestant king William of Orange. Often referred to as "Unionists," because they desire to remain in union with the United Kingdom.

Ulster. The traditional name for the northern part of Ireland, which includes both Northern Ireland and several counties of the Republic. Today, though, the name is used for Northern Ireland and often indicates the Troubles that have beset the region.

and churches seem to be held together by green ivy that now twines around them.

A New Ireland

As the twenty-first century began, Ireland could see the end of a terrible era. For 160 years, the Irish had been sorrowfully leaving the island to seek their fortunes in places with more jobs and opportunity. The population of the island had dropped from a high of 8.5 million in 1840 to 2.8 million people, many living in poverty, in the Republic in the 1960s.

A street musician performs with bagpipes.

Even in the 1980s, young people were still leaving Ireland, needing to earn a living but afraid that they could never return to Ireland and earn a good living. Then the high-tech computer age found Ireland and its well-educated people. Opportunity abounded, and many people who had left in the 1980s returned home joyfully.

Today, everyone wants to be part of Ireland. Irishness is celebrated. The island's theaters, music, dance, folklore, and literature are an essential part of European and American culture. The Republic's economic growth is the envy of the world. The ancient island is a bright spot in the twenty-first century.

Braving the Atlantic

IRELAND STANDS ALONE, FACING THE WAVES, WINDS, AND isolation of the North Atlantic Ocean. The rock cliffs and crags of the Irish coast bear the brunt of the island's position as the outpost of Europe.

Ptolemy, a Greek geographer in ancient times, wrote a description of Ireland, probably by assembling information from sailors. For them, Ireland was on the edge of the known world. They called the island *Ierne*, which eventually became both *Éire*—the Irish name of the Republic of Ireland—and *Hibernia*, an old name for the island that isn't used much anymore.

Opposite: **The Cliffs of Moher tower high above the Atlantic.**

The Ice-Covered Island

The entire island of Ireland is 32,595 square miles (84,421 square kilometers) in area. The Republic of Ireland occupies 27,136 square miles (70,282 sq km), about 83 percent of the island. Northern Ireland, a province of the United Kingdom, covers 5,459 square miles (14,139 sq km). The island is 302 miles (486 km) at its greatest length and 171 miles (275 km) at its greatest width.

The island is shaped rather like a saucer, with a lowland area in the middle and mountains forming a raised outer edge, though the mountains are not continuous. None of the mountains are particularly rough—they were smoothed by glaciers in the distant past.

Ireland and the Atlantic

The first successful transatlantic telegraph cable was laid in 1866, from Valentia Island, off the coast of Kerry, to Newfoundland. This enterprise was backed by American Cyrus Field and Irish-born scientist Lord Kelvin.

Cobh (pictured), the port area east of Cork, was the last port of call of the great ocean liner *Titanic* on its fateful maiden voyage of 1912. The liner sank after striking an iceberg. On May 7, 1915, the passenger ship *Lusitania* was sunk by a German submarine off Cobh. The deaths of more than 1,000 people encouraged the United States to join in fighting World War I (1914–1918) in 1917.

In 1919, the first nonstop flight across the Atlantic Ocean was made by British aviators John Alcock and Arthur Brown. They took off from Newfoundland, in Canada, on June 14 and landed—or crashed—the next day in a bog near Clifden in Galway.

During World War II (1939–1945), one of the primary means of transport between Europe and the United

States were the flying boats that went from Foynes in County Limerick. A museum is now based in their original terminal building. Some people say that Irish coffee originated in a coffee shop at the airport in 1943.

Until the last great Ice Age, which ended about 10,000 years ago, Ireland and Great Britain were attached to the European continent. When the glaciers melted, the water level of the surrounding ocean rose enough to fill the low-lying regions. Great Britain was separated from mainland Europe, and Ireland from Great Britain. The Irish Sea lies between Ireland and Great Britain. It varies between 11 and 120 miles (18 and 193 km) in width. The entire island of Ireland has a coastline of 3,500 miles (5,633 km).

Ireland's Geographical Features

Area: Ireland: 32,595 square miles (84,421 sq km) [Republic of Ireland: 27,136 square miles (70,282 sq km); Northern Ireland: 5,459 square miles (14,139 sq km)]

Highest Elevation: Carrantuohill, 3,414 feet (1,041 m) above sea level, in Macgillicuddy's Reeks, Republic of Ireland

Lowest Elevation: 1.3 feet (0.4 m) below sea level at The Marsh near Downpatrick, Northern Ireland

Coastline: 3,500 miles (5,633 km)

Greatest Distance North to South: 302 miles (486 km)

Greatest Distance East to West: 171 miles (275 km)

Longest River: Shannon, 240 miles (386 km)

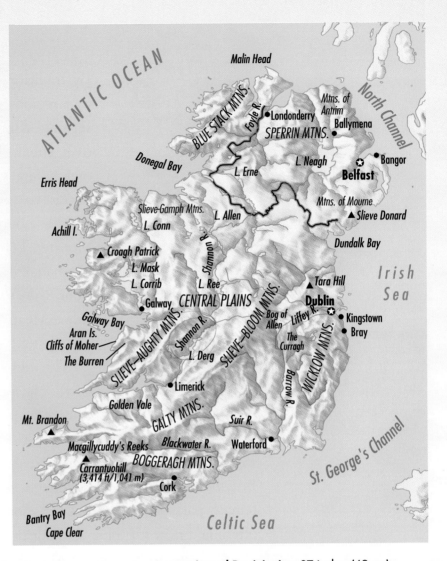

Largest Island: Achill Island, 56 square miles (145 sq km)

Largest Lake: Lough Neagh, 147 square miles (381 sq km)

Greatest Annual Precipitation: 60 inches (152 centimeters) in the southwest

Lowest Annual Precipitation: 27 inches (69 cm) in the east

Lowest Annual Average Temperature: 35°F (2°C) on eastern coast of Northern Ireland in January

Highest Annual Average Temperature: 61°F (16°C) in Belfast and Cork in July

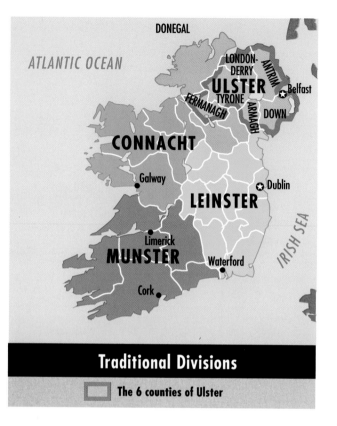

Traditional Divisions

The 6 counties of Ulster

By tradition, Ireland is divided into four regions that were once ruled by separate kings, with one high king over them. The names of the four regions are still used in the popular mind to indicate various parts of the country. They are Ulster, Munster, Leinster, and Connacht (or Connaught). The *ster* ending came from the Vikings. A fifth region, called Meath, is now regarded as part of Leinster.

The old region of Ulster, in the north, consisted of nine counties. But when the people were choosing, in 1920, whether to belong to the Irish Free State or Northern Ireland, only Antrim, Derry (called Londonderry by the British), Tyrone, Down, Armagh, and Fermanagh chose to remain part of the United Kingdom. The name "Ulster" is often used now for those six counties.

Peninsulas and Islands

The island has a jagged coast, especially in the west, where the peninsulas jut out into the Atlantic. There is a series of three rugged and beautiful peninsulas on the southwest coast. Iveragh, the center peninsula, is made famous by the Ring of Kerry. Though sounding like some ancient site created by

The Ring of Kerry

humans long ago, the ring is a beautiful new road that circles the peninsula. Almost all visitors to Ireland make the journey around the ring, which is 112 miles (180 km) long.

North of Iveragh and divided from it by Dingle Bay is Dingle Peninsula. South of it is Beara Peninsula, which is much more rugged and isolated. South of Beara is Bantry Bay.

Off each peninsula are small islands. Some of them, such as the Blaskets off Dingle, were populated for centuries by families living lives of great isolation. In 1953, the families

View of Blasket Islands from Dingle Peninsula

rejected the isolation and moved to the mainland. Most Irish children read Peig Sayer's book *Peig*, which tells the bleak story of life on the islands. The Blaskets are probably going to be protected as a national park.

The largest island lies off the coast of County Mayo. Achill, at 56 square miles (145 sq km), features cliffs,

huge rocks, and dramatic moorland. South of Achill is Clare Island, best known as the home of pirate Grace O'Malley. The daughter of "sea rovers"—a polite name for pirates—Graánne Ní Mháille took her greatest pleasure in harassing the ships of Queen Elizabeth I of England.

Perhaps the most famous islands are the three very isolated Aran Islands—Inishmore, Inishmaan, and Inisheer—which lie off Galway. Today, the islands can be reached by ferries or airplanes, but visitors may not bring cars with them.

North of Kerry is County Clare's rocky and spectacular coast. One of the most famous sites in Ireland are the Cliffs of Moher. For a distance of 5 miles (8 km), the land ends in a sheer drop of 650 feet (198 meters) to the sea. Just inland from the cliffs is the strange limestone feature called the Burren. The west, especially County Mayo, has few visitors, despite the fact that it and its neighbor Connemara feature beautiful sea cliffs, flower-filled bogs, and charming lakes.

Looking at the Republic's Cities

Cork is the Republic of Ireland's second-largest city. It is located at the mouth of the Lee River in southern Ireland. The city began as monastery in the A.D. 600s. Today Cork is the major seaport of southern Ireland. Important industries in Cork include making leather goods, beer, and spirits. University College Cork attracts many students. More than 50,000 visitors jam the city each October for the Cork Jazz Festival and the Cork Film Festival.

The Republic's third-largest city is Limerick. This seaport town is on the Shannon River in southwestern Ireland. Vikings settled the area in the 800s. Today Limerick is known for its lace making, creameries, and flour mills. The city's oldest building is St. Mary's Cathedral, founded in 1172. Visitors learn about Irish history at the Limerick Museum and the Hunt Museum.

The fourth-largest city of the Republic is Galway (pictured). This western Ireland city is located northwest of Limerick, on Galway Bay. Before the 1200s, Galway was an important fishing village. Fishing is still a big business there, but the electronics and textile industries have grown in importance. University College Galway is a center of Gaelic culture. Many of its students study the Gaelic language. Throughout the year, thousands of Irish people and visitors from other countries travel to Galway. They enjoy the Jazz Festival in February; the Poetry and Literature Festival in April; and the Galway Film Festival, the Galway Arts Festival, and the Galway Race Week in July.

Waterford is the fifth-largest city. Located on the Suir River in southeastern Ireland, it is an important port. Settled by the Vikings in the 700s, it is best known today for its beautiful Waterford crystal. Each year, thousands of people tour the Waterford Crystal Factory and watch glassblowers, cutters, and engravers as they make bowls, glasses, and ornaments. Visitors also enjoy walking the city's narrow streets and alleyways to see Christ Church Cathedral, Blackfriars Abbey, and The Granary, a new museum.

The Strange Burren

One of the most unusual natural sites in Ireland is called the Burren, in County Clare. The Irish word *boireann* means "rocky land." The Burren is a 50-square-mile (129-sq-km) raised dome of limestone with little vegetation on its sloping sides. A number of caves that were carved out by ancient rivers are found within the Burren. Aillwee Cave features beautiful formations and an underground waterfall.

There are no trees on the Burren, because tree roots cannot dig down into the limestone. There are, however, pockets of grass where soil has accumulated in the cracks and crevices of the limestone. Within these pockets are small cottages that were once inhabited. Even more-ancient stone monuments and tombs have been found in the Burren. The vegetation of this limestone national park includes many alpine (high-altitude) species that are found nowhere else.

The Shannon River

Lakes and Rivers

The Shannon is Ireland's longest river—240 miles (386 km). It rises in County Cavan, northwest of Dublin. Starting in the eighteenth century, the Grand Canal and the Royal Canal were built connecting Dublin to the Shannon and thus to places farther west. These canals fell into disuse but were reopened for transportation—primarily pleasure boats—in the 1960s.

The lower Shannon is bordered by pastureland, making this an important dairy region. The Shannon widens at several places into lakes, or loughs. The largest is Lough Derg. As might be expected with a major river, there are wetlands along the Shannon. These attract many birds and other animals.

The largest lake in Ireland—actually, the largest lake in the British Isles—is Lough Neagh, west of Belfast. It is 147 square miles (381 sq km) in area but seems even larger because it is surrounded by inaccessible marshland. Legend says that the giant Finn MacCool formed Lough Neagh by grabbing a huge handful of turf and flinging it into the sea, where it formed the Isle of Man.

Torc Waterfall in Killarney National Park

Killarney National Park was developed around Muckross House and Gardens. The spectacular scenery features Lough Leane, a popular lake for sailing, which is surrounded by mountains. Muckross House was built in the mid-1800s as a country estate and was given to the nation, along with 11,000 acres (4,452 hectares). The park was later doubled in size.

The Giant's Causeway

Finn MacCool, the warrior giant of Irish myth, yearned to see his girlfriend, who lived on Staffa, one of the western islands off Scotland. To keep his lady love's feet dry on her journey, legend has it, he constructed a special walkway connecting County Antrim in Northern Ireland with Scotland. This walkway became Ireland's most striking sight, the Giant's Causeway.

A causeway is a raised land bridge across a body of water. This one is an unusual mass of six-sided columns—perhaps 37,000 of them—of basalt rock from ancient lava flows. They've been eroded by the sea and ice into a stunning pathway through the water to Staffa. The United Nations has designated the Giant's Causeway as a World Heritage Site.

Mountains and Tradition

The mountains of Ireland would not be much more than hills in some countries, but they are quite beautiful and attractive to walkers. The highest point in Ireland is Carrantuohill, at 3,414 feet (1,041 m). It is part of the range called Macgillicuddy's Reeks in Killarney. The mountains are named for Macgillicuddy, a man who once owned the mountains.

Mount Brandon on Dingle Peninsula is the nation's second-highest mountain. On St. Brendan's Day, May 16, people climb Mount Brandon along an ancient track called the Saint's Road.

Standing stone with Macgillicuddy's Reeks in the background

The Wicklow region south of Dublin is called the Garden of Ireland. Irishmen who were wanted by the law used to hide out in the Wicklow Mountains. Today, it is to this region that Dubliners go to hike and picnic.

The Mountains of Mourne in County Down south of Newcastle in Northern Ireland are a group of low, rounded hills. The Glens of Antrim are not nearly so gentle. A series of nine glens, or isolated valleys, they were created by the retreat of the glaciers long ago, as the waters ran off the northern end of the island. In the glens, the water still pours down in the form of waterfalls. The glens are surrounded by bogland and are hard to reach. Many Irish fairy tales tell of mystical events in the glens.

A farm nestled in the Mountains of Mourne

The Temperate Island

A farmer carries a full bucket after milking his cows in the rain.

Gerald, a Welsh visitor in the late 1100s, wrote: "Ireland is the most temperate of all countries. Snow is seldom, and lasts only for a short time. There is such a plentiful supply of rain, such an ever-present overhanging of clouds and fog, that summer scarcely gives three consecutive days of really fine weather. . . . The country enjoys the freshness and mildness of spring almost all the year round."

The island enjoys a complete mix of weather, but little of it is terrible. The Gulf Stream, the main warm current that crosses the Atlantic from the Caribbean, keeps the climate of Ireland mild, though quite wet. The southwest gets about 55 inches (140 cm) of rain each year, while the east gets only about half that. The central part receives about 31 to 47 inches (79 to 119 cm) of rain each year. Rain is distributed quite evenly throughout the island and the year. Ireland rarely gets snow except on the higher elevations, where it quickly melts.

Bogs and Peat

The low central plain, which is made up of glacier-deposited clay, is the site of many bogs. Clay keeps water from draining from the land. Bogs formed where plants died and settled into low-lying lakes thousands of years ago. Year after year, dead plants collapsed into the water and failed to decompose. Over the centuries, the lakes were filled in by the plants, turning into bogs.

Why didn't the plants decompose? Because of the primary living plant of bogs, a moss called sphagnum. Sphagnum moss has large holes in the cells that open to the outside of the plant tissue. These holes hold so much water that air doesn't get into the bog water beyond the top few inches. Bacteria and fungi, which normally make plants decompose, do not get enough oxygen to survive and do their work. The dead plants are gradually compressed into a material called peat, or turf. Peat can be removed, drained of water, and used as a fuel in fires. Several community power plants in Ireland burn peat to produce electricity.

About 17 percent of Ireland is covered by bogs. People who own bog land today often harvest the sphagnum moss and sell it to garden shops. When sphagnum is mixed with soil, the soil holds water much longer than soil without the moss.

Gathering peat from a bog

Some Irish people are trying to preserve bogs, especially because the bogs serve as habitat for wildlife. Nine species of dragonflies are found hovering over the bogs. A flit of color may indicate the presence of one of the two rare types of butterfly associated with bogs.

Since ancient times, wooden pathways have been built through the bogs. Anyone hiding from the law had to know the safe routes through, or they would have been caught in the marshy ground and died there. Folktales say that people have been lured by fairy lights from the safety of the wooden walk-ways into danger.

Living Things

Until about 10,000 years ago, the island of Ireland was attached to the island of Great Britain, which was itself attached to mainland Europe. Only briefly after the last glacial period did animals have a chance to move westward into Ireland. Some, such as most reptiles, never made it to Ireland before the sea rose, separating the islands. Most of the plant species of Europe failed to reach Ireland.

Forests occupy about 8 percent of the land area. Southern Ireland had huge forests of oak trees until the 1600s, when the English landlords began to cut them down to create fields. They exported oak, ash, and elm wood to England. The forested area was down to only 1 percent at the time of independence in 1921. One of the first missions of the Irish Free State was to replant trees to protect the land from erosion.

Sacred Trees

Since ancient times, certain trees have been regarded as sacred in Ireland. Two of them have red berries—rowan (mountain ash) and holly. The blackthorn is a white-flowered hedge plant of the rose family. Most important, though, was the oak. The name *druid*, for a learned priest of the ancient Celts, meant "knowing the oak tree." Druidic rituals were carried out in oak forests.

Today, tradition holds that the hawthorn tree (branch pictured) is likely to be home to some fairies, so it's bad luck to cut one down. Gnarled hawthorn sticks called shillelaghs, associated with the Irish because of their prominence in British and American movies, are often sold to tourists as "genuine Irish weapons."

Animals

There are thirty-one species of mammals native to Ireland, though most are shared with Europe. They are primarily of the smaller varieties, such as the Irish hare, which is brown with white ears. Once, Ireland was the home of many bears, but they have been gone for two hundred years, as have the wolves. Foxes and badgers still hide in woods. Weasels and moles, like snakes, have never lived in Ireland, though pine martens do.

Glenveagh National Park in the far north is home to a herd of red deer, which are not native but introduced. Red deer have been moved onto the Blasket Islands.

Some whales and sharks feed off the coast of Ireland when they are on their way north for the summer. They can sometimes be seen from the Cliffs of Moher. Seals and sea lions may adorn the rocks along the coasts. Otters, too, live along the seacoast and occasionally swim into the rivers.

Ireland has a hundred or more of its own bird species that nest on the island, but almost three times as many species visit the island while migrating between Africa, the Mediterranean, and the Arctic. A wildlife preserve in County Wexford is the winter home of three-quarters of the world's population of the Greenland white-fronted goose.

Irish Ponies and Horses

The British Isles have several breeds of ponies, but the one from Connemara (pictured) is the largest and the only pony native to Ireland. This long-necked pony has short legs but is very surefooted on rough ground. Legend says that this pony's ancestors mated with Spanish horses that swam from ships of the Spanish Armada, which crashed on the rocky western coast. The Irish draught (or draft) horse is a workhorse that was bred in the 1800s to be a combination of worker, hunter, and handsome family horse. It was mixed with the Thoroughbred, producing the Irish hunter or Irish sport horse.

An osprey holds its prey.

Rathlin Island in Northern Ireland has only a few human inhabitants, but it is home to thousands of graceful seabirds such as puffins, kittiwakes, razorbills, and guillemots. Ospreys nest in the area of southern Ireland called Eagle Rock.

Some people say that the world's last great auk was killed on the Saltee Islands off the Irish coast in 1845. Others, though, hold that it died a year earlier, off Iceland. These big birds, related to puffins, used to be one of the major large birds of the world, but they were tasty prey.

Ireland has only one reptile, a small lizard. No snakes reached the island from Europe, though a strong tradition holds that they lived there until St. Patrick drove them away. The story says that at Croagh Patrick, a mountain in Mayo, he rang a bell. At the sound of it, the snakes threw themselves into the sea.

Perhaps eels are the substitute for snakes. These long, thin fish, which are great eating, hatch in the Sargasso Sea, part of the North Atlantic. They swim across the ocean, heading for the rivers and streams of Ireland. Lough Neagh in particular is known for its eel fishing.

An eel

The Irish and Their Dogs

Ireland may have produced more breeds of dogs than any other country of comparable size. At least five of these canines, bred in the mid-nineteenth century, are popular the world over.

The Irish setter (pictured) is a large, sleek dog with coppery red hair. This hunter was originally both red and white but is now only red.

The Irish wolfhound is one of the largest dogs. When perched on its hind legs, it stands taller than a man. It can weigh up to 200 pounds (90 kilograms).

Two terriers—energetic, usually small hunting dogs—are the Irish and the Kerry blue. The Irish terrier is one of the oldest breeds in Ireland. It has a solid reddish wiry coat. The Kerry blue has a very curly, steel-blue coat.

The Irish water spaniel is indeed a water-loving dog, eager to dive into water and retrieve a bird for a hunter. The water slides off its liver-colored curly coat. This dog has been known since about the 1100s.

One People

THE FIRST HUMANS ARRIVED IN IRELAND IN THE CENTURIES after the separation of the islands of Great Britain and Ireland (also called Little Britain), about 8,000 years ago. Perhaps they came from Scotland as small bands of hunter-gatherers. They lived in temporary huts, hunting wild boar and small mammals.

About 4,000 years later, farming folk arrived. These people may have come from farther south, through France, perhaps even from the Mediterranean regions.

The foundation of a house made of logs was found at Ballynagilly in County Tyrone in 1967. It had been built at least 5,000 years before. The farmer probably kept domesticated animals and had cleared forests for his fields.

Opposite: **Ruins from the Stone Age on Achill Island**

NORTH SEA

IRELAND

ENGLAND

NETHERLANDS

ATLANTIC OCEAN

English Channel

FRANCE

Land Bridge 6,000 Years Ago

Ancient land

Present land

Finding Their Graves

Not long after farming was begun in County Tyrone, various communities throughout the north built what came to be called court graves. These consisted of small stone chambers surrounding an open, probably semicircular, area where burial ceremonies took place. Later graves are called *dolmens*. They are visible today as two tall stones with a flat stone raised on top. When built, they had soil packed around the stones.

Passage graves are found farther south. Centered in the Boyne Valley of County Meath, they were built underground. The bodies of the dead were cremated, or burned to ashes. A ceremony was held in a chamber at the end of a long passage. The most complete passage grave is at Newgrange, northwest of Dublin. Circle designs found in the chamber have become symbols of ancient Ireland. A similar, though smaller, passage grave is found at nearby Knowth.

About a thousand years passed before another group of people arrived from Europe. Called the Beaker Folk, these people are known today primarily by the pottery jars, or beakers, they made. They also built graves that are similar to ones found in France.

The Celts Across Europe

Celtic Territories by A.D. Third Century

The Coming of the Celts

The Celts were a people who probably originated in central Europe. About 3,000 years ago, they began to spread out. They came to Britain and Ireland in three waves of migration. The first group has been called Scotia Celts. They moved on to northern Great Britain and started Scotland. The second group were the Britons, who also founded Britanny in France and gave their name to Britain. The third were the Gaels, whose descendants still live in Ireland.

In most regions of the continent, Celtic cultures were overwhelmed by the Roman Empire, which flourished from 27 B.C. to about A.D. 400. However, the Romans left the native people of Ireland alone. Gold artifacts and extraordinary art from this time, called Celtic, have come down to us today. The Romans called Ireland *Hibernia.*

The early Celts were iron users who lived in small communities on easily defended hills. They built stone walls, now called ring forts, around their villages. Numerous ring forts still stand. The Celts had no written language, and so little has come down to us today to tell us how they lived or what they thought.

The Coming of Christianity

About A.D. 400, when Romans were withdrawing from Great Britain, a sixteen-year-old lad who lived near the western coast of Britain was kidnapped by raiders from Ireland. His name was Patrick, and he spent six years on Ireland as a slave before he was able to escape. This man later returned to Ireland to teach the Celts about Jesus Christ.

All we know about the man, who became St. Patrick, the Patron Saint of Ireland, comes from his own writing, *The Confession.* He traveled throughout Ireland for years, spreading the gospel of Christianity, baptizing those who converted.

Also regarded as a founder of the Irish Church was Palladius, a bishop sent by Pope Celestine (the leader of the Roman Catholic Church) about A.D. 431 to establish the

Christian Church on the distant island. But nothing is known about Palladius or the success of his mission.

No matter who did the missionary work, it could not have been an easy task. Ireland of the time had no big towns. There were many small communities of people, called *tuatha*. Each tuath, or clan, was controlled by a warrior-king chosen by the people. A missionary would have had to approach each tuath separately to convert the people to Christianity.

Many of the new Christians joined other believers in communities called monasteries. Monasteries became the center of religion, power, and learning for the next several hundred years. They attracted Christians from all over Europe, as Ireland became the island of "scholars and saints."

Irish monks copied
manuscripts by hand.

The Saintly Traveler

One of St. Patrick's most significant followers was Brendan of Clonfert. Tradition holds that Brendan—later known as St. Brendan—made voyages out into the North Atlantic in a small boat. According to the legends that were recorded as early as the eighth century, one trip took him to a land that could have been North America.

For centuries, the idea that St. Brendan could have made such a trip was laughed at. But in June 1977, English adventurer Tim Severin sailed a small leather-sided boat to Iceland and then to Greenland, showing that Brendan might truly have been the European discoverer of North America. Severin's boat is on exhibit at Craggaunowen.

An estimated 150 tuatha began to merge into five groups of tuatha—called fifths—each with a king over it. The fifths were Ulster in the north, Connacht in the west, Munster in the south, Leinster in the east, and Meath, or Mide, between Ulster and Leinster.

Each of these fifths had families that became the important leaders. Gradually, one leader came to be regarded as the high king. Often, he belonged to the *Uí Neill* (later O Neill or O'Neill) clan, with headquarters on a hill called Tara in Meath.

The big landowners supported the abbots and abbesses who ran the monasteries. Much of the country's wealth was concentrated in the Church. Sometimes one family would invade and destroy the monasteries of other families, who

Tara of the High Kings

The kings of Ireland were at the height of power when St. Patrick was turning them and their followers from paganism to Christianity. Located on the hill of Tara was a castle with a huge banquet hall, where the high kings entertained in splendor. Legend says that St. Patrick visited the king at Tara on Easter Sunday and worked a miracle that kept him from being poisoned by a Druid priest. The king, impressed, converted to Christianity. Whatever remained of Tara's walls disappeared in the nineteenth century. The Stone of Destiny, a massive rock used for the coronations of Tara's kings, endures.

would try to get revenge. They stopped fighting each other and banded together when invaders from outside arrived and attacked the monasteries and churches.

They Came from Scandinavia

As Ireland became famed for its monasteries, wealthy European families began to send their sons to Ireland. They brought with them great gifts of gold and jewels. It was this wealth that the marauding Vikings from Scandinavia were seeking when they began to sail up the rivers of Ireland.

A Viking ship

Probably the first landing by Vikings on Irish territory took place on Lambay Island near Dublin in 795. Church properties quickly became the target of many raids. Some Vikings, however, found Ireland a lovely place and settled down to trade and raise families. These Norsemen founded trading centers that became Ireland's first cities—Dublin, Waterford, Limerick, and Cork.

For two hundred years, the Vikings controlled Ireland. But Brian Bórú, a High King, put an end to their power. In 1014, the forces of Brian fought the Battle of Clontarf against the united troops of Norse-founded Dublin and the king of Leinster, who hoped to displace Brian. Brian's troops were

Irish king Brian Bórú was killed after defeating the Vikings.

unexpectedly powerful, and they won the day. After the battle, the old warrior was at prayer when an enemy stabbed him in the back. Though he was murdered, he had broken the power of the Vikings in Ireland. These Scandinavians quietly merged into the Irish population.

They Came from England

In 1066, soldiers from Normandy in France conquered England, and William, called the Conqueror, became king of

England. For a hundred years, the Normans ignored Ireland, thinking—as the Romans had thought—that it was not worth bothering about.

Then Dermot MacMurrough, who had been sent into exile in Britain by High King Rory O'Connor, hoped to regain his throne as king of Leinster. He brought with him from Wales some Anglo-Norman knights to help him. Chief among MacMurrough's supporters was Richard de Clare, the Earl of Pembroke, who came to be called Strongbow.

Rory O'Connor was unable to stop Strongbow's forces. He went into history as Ireland's last high king. But then a different king, Henry II of England, took over.

As Henry II saw Strongbow's conquests of Ireland, he began to worry about the possibility of a strong kingdom developing across the Irish Sea. In 1171, the king himself came to Ireland to lead his troops against Strongbow and the Irish.

The English quickly took control of Ireland. The king gave his knights land to own and protect. Some knights, especially John de Courcy, destroyed monasteries because of the hold the religious leaders had on the people. De Courcy built new monasteries, which he peopled with monks from England. His castle, Carrickfergus in Antrim, remains one of the best-preserved castles in Ireland.

In the early 1200s, King John of England did not want his knights to become strong, so his personal troops invaded and took control of some of these new castles. John divided up the land according to his whims. His people took charge of agriculture, draining bogland, and building prosperous farms.

Most of the knights' estates included about 3,000 acres (1,214 ha). The lord often built a castle on the high ground, surrounded by a moat. The ruins of many of them are still visible; a few are still lived in. The Irish, who had once owned the land, now found themselves tenants, working for the lord of the manor and able to plow and plant for themselves only a small strip of land. The leaders of the ancient kingdoms became mere chieftains under the Anglo-Normans.

The Coming of the Protestants

For several centuries, Ireland was ruled for the English king by the Earls of Kildare. In the 1530s, King Henry VIII of England broke with the Roman Catholic Church in order to divorce his wife and remarry, hoping to have sons. He established the Protestant Church of England, setting out on a course that left Catholics in the British Isles at a disadvantage for hundreds of years. When the Kildares tried to encourage a rebellion

This old illustration shows a battle between Irish and English forces in 1577.

against the king, Henry's troops fought back, destroying monasteries and taking away the lands of the rebels.

When Henry's daughter Elizabeth, an avowed Protestant, became queen, the pope decreed that the Irish Catholics did not owe her allegiance. She became the enemy of the Irish, so the Irish called on Elizabeth's enemies, especially the Spanish and the pope, to help them.

In 1588, Spain, for a number of reasons—not just to help Catholic Ireland—sent a huge fleet of ships, the Armada, to attack England. Driven off by both bad weather and Elizabeth's powerful naval force, some Spanish ships sailed for Ireland. Many of them were forced onto the rocks of the coast. Thousands of Spanish sailors drowned. Many Spanish sailors made it to land, however. Those who were not murdered by English soldiers settled into villages, married, and added dark Spanish physical characteristics to the Irish appearance.

The English confiscated almost 4 million acres (1.6 million ha) of land belonging to the rebel leaders. Part of this land in the north was so rocky that it was useless for agriculture. This useless land was granted to the Irish

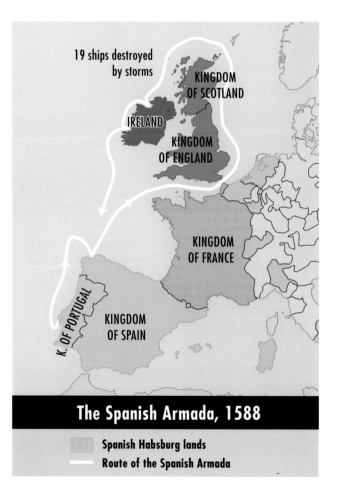

19 ships destroyed by storms

KINGDOM OF SCOTLAND

IRELAND

KINGDOM OF ENGLAND

KINGDOM OF FRANCE

K. OF PORTUGAL

KINGDOM OF SPAIN

The Spanish Armada, 1588

Spanish Habsburg lands
Route of the Spanish Armada

to live on. The good land was kept by the English government for granting as plantations to Protestant settlers from England and Scotland. Eventually, most of this region became Northern Ireland.

Not only did the Irish lose their land, but many of them also lost their country. During the 1650s, while Protestant Oliver Cromwell ruled Britain as Lord Protector, more than 100,000 Catholic Irishmen were transported (sent as prisoners) to England's North American colonies.

The Penal Laws

King James II of England, a Catholic, tried to introduce religious toleration, but the Protestants feared such a move. They persuaded Parliament to invite James's son-in-law, Protestant King William of Orange, and William's wife,

King William III (William of Orange) defeats King James II at the Battle of the Boyne.

Mary, to become the British monarchs. James was forced to give up his throne in 1688, and he fled to Ireland to raise an army that would help him regain power. In 1690, however, King William himself led his troops into Ireland, where in the Battle of the Boyne, the Protestants, or Orangemen, gained control of Ireland.

In 1695, the Irish parliament, which was Protestant, persuaded King William to sign the Penal Laws. These laws removed all political rights from Irish Catholics.

Catholics were forbidden to carry weapons. They could attend Mass in their own churches, but they could not inherit land or send their children to mainland Europe for a Catholic education. When a Catholic landowner died, laws required that the land be divided among his sons, unless the oldest son turned Protestant. Any Catholics who retained money were prevented from buying land. Gradually, any land owned by Catholics was divided into smaller and smaller plots. Catholic Irish farmers who were unable to pay their rent on the small farms they were allotted on the Protestants' property were often evicted. Remains of the destroyed cottages still stand as testimony to a terrible period in Irish history.

This takeover by Protestants in Ireland is called the Ascendancy. The Protestant Ascendancy remained in control for two hundred years.

Rebellion Against the Ascendancy

The Irish were always on the verge of rebelling. Secret societies were formed, dedicated to independence for the Irish and equal rights for Catholics. They were often just as cruel to the Irish who seemed to give in to the English as they were to the English. In Dublin, an organization called the Defenders grew among Catholics, and in response, a Protestant group called the Orange Order was founded in 1795.

It Might Have Worked

From 1782 to 1800, England let Ireland rule itself with a parliament in Dublin. The leader of the nationalist movement that forced the issue was a Protestant named Henry Grattan, and the parliament was soon called Grattan's Parliament. However, he was slow to demand that England grant Ireland full independence. When the radical societies turned to violence, England put Ireland under tight control. The parliament was disbanded.

The Act of Union

An organization called the United Irishmen was formed to bring Catholics and Protestants together to create an independent, nonreligious Ireland. But soon they were concentrating on the rights of Catholics. The Defenders and the United Irishmen merged their efforts in an uprising of 1798. They succeeded in getting some help from France, but bad weather drove French ships away from Ireland. The Irish leader of the sympathetic French forces, Wolfe Tone, was caught and sentenced to be hanged by the English, but he committed suicide.

Irish leader, Wolfe Tone

Rebellion spread, and more troops were brought from England. Villages were taken over or burned by both sides in the struggle. In England, the government, fearing that the Ascendancy was unable to rule, took direct control of the island. The English parliament passed the Act of Union in 1800. This created a new United Kingdom, bringing together under one government England, Scotland, Wales, and Ireland, all controlled from London.

Most Anglo-Irish Protestants liked the union. Many Irish Catholics of the elite also supported it because they hoped that the act would lead to repeal of laws that kept Catholics from serving in Parliament. But they were wrong. The act led only to tighter controls on Catholics. Thousands of Irish Catholics left each year for North America.

A Hero in the Streets

The main street of many Irish towns is called O'Connell Street. These streets are named for the Irish hero Daniel O'Connell. Born near Cahirciveen in County Kerry in 1775, he was a young man, just qualified to be a lawyer, when the English parliament passed the Act of Union in 1800. He dedicated his life to getting it repealed. Though elected to Parliament, he was refused his seat because of his religion.

Even after the Catholic Emancipation Act was passed in 1829, he realized that Parliament would never allow the Irish to be Irish. He began to speak out at mass meetings against the Act of Union. In 1841, he became the first Catholic lord mayor of Dublin. The English viewed O'Connell as a traitor, and in 1843, he was sent to prison for a few months. That episode destroyed his health. He sailed to Italy, hoping to improve it, but he died in 1847. His body was buried in Dublin, but his heart was sent to Rome. He has since been known as the Liberator.

Catholic lawyer Daniel O'Connell led the fight for freedom for Catholics. His success led the British prime minister, the Duke of Wellington, to get Parliament to pass the Catholic Emancipation Act in 1829. That act canceled the old Penal Acts and allowed Catholic Irishmen the right to become members of the English parliament. Soon, though, the Irish entered another dreadful period that would change the face of Ireland forever.

Over the centuries, the Irish had become tenants, or renters, on the land that they should have owned. And on the meager plots they were allowed to keep, the only feasible crop was potatoes. The summer of 1845 was terribly wet, and a fungus attacked the potato crop. The fungus returned even stronger the next year. More fields were infested, and people starved. There was no cure for this blight except time itself and long periods of dry weather. The cure took six years.

The Irish no longer call this terrible period the Irish Famine. Instead, they call it the Great Hunger, because the word "famine" implies that it was a natural event related to only land and weather. In fact, there was plenty of food other than potatoes, but the English controlled it. They continued to export this food to England while a million Irish people died of starvation.

A priest visits the home of a starving family.

For the equivalent of $10 in U.S. currency, an Irishman could sail to the United States. Passage to Canada was even cheaper. The ships sailed from any Irish port where people gathered looking for passage. Though ships previously had sailed only in spring and summer, many immigrant ships crossed in winter, weighed down by ice and blasted by terrible winds. The journey lasted at least four weeks, and bad weather could make it last twice that long.

After the first year of the famine, the terrible disease typhus stalked the emigrant ships. Thousands died without

A statue in Cobb, County Cork honors those who left Ireland during the Great Hunger.

ever reaching their destination. The vessels carrying the doomed passengers came to be called coffin ships. Amazingly, only fifty ships went down at sea during the hundreds of famine voyages.

Many ships went to Canada, carrying people who were put on board by landlords who cared nothing for their tenants' desires. They simply wanted to be rid of any responsibility for them. Because landlords were required to pay taxes on their tenants, it was cheaper to ship them away than pay the taxes.

A New Kind of Fight

The Great Hunger ended when the blight eased and crops could be grown again. Landlords had discovered by then, however, that it was cheaper to do without their tenant farmers. Some people who were evicted founded the Irish Republican Brotherhood (IRB) in 1858. This group of revolutionaries was popularly known as the Fenians, which comes from the Fianna Éireann, the Irish warriors of legend who were led by Fionn MacCumhaill, or MacCool.

The evictions were eventually stopped, but during the years following there were increasing calls for independence, or at least justice. People in both England and Ireland decided that Home Rule had to be brought about, that the Irish should make decisions affecting the Irish. However, those favoring Home Rule were so shocked by the scandal caused by Charles Stewart Parnell, an Irish Home Rule leader, that they split. Home Rule was voted down in 1886.

The Parnell Scandal

Charles Stewart Parnell, born in 1846 in Avondale, County Wicklow, to an American woman, was a Protestant who supported the rights of the Irish tenant farmers and even went to jail for their sake and for the sake of Home Rule. In 1885, his political party gained eighty-five seats in the House of Commons, and he acquired the nickname The Uncrowned King. But his support eroded quickly when it was announced in the newspapers that he had been living with Kitty O'Shea, the wife of another man. Parnell was voted out of power. He died in 1891.

In 1914, the English parliament approved Home Rule. The act called for a two-part Ireland (Protestant and Catholic), both owing allegiance to the British Crown. But it was too late. The fighting in Europe that would become World War I had started, and Parliament put Home Rule on hold until after the war. By then, a different war had started in Ireland.

The Easter Rising

Members of the IRB decided that if Germany was England's enemy in the European war, perhaps Germany would help Ireland fight for its independence from England. No arms reached Ireland from Germany, but the IRB and some other volunteers formed a Citizens' Army, which went ahead with plans to declare independence.

On the day after Easter in 1916, posters of a proclamation were nailed up in Dublin. The proclamation read:

The Provisional Government of the Irish Republic to the People of Ireland:

Irishmen and Irishwomen: In the name of God and of the dead generations from which she receives her old tradition of nationhood, through us, summons her children to the flag and strikes for her freedom.... In every generation the Irish people have asserted their right to national freedom and sovereignty; six times during the past three hundred years they have asserted it in arms. Standing on that fundamental right and again asserting it in arms in the face of the world, we hereby proclaim the Irish Republic as a Sovereign Independent State....

Soldiers and civilians shoot at each other.

A three-color flag appeared over the General Post Office in Dublin, but most Dubliners first learned of the Easter Rising when the fighting began in the streets. The bloodshed lasted a week, with more than 500 people killed before the IRB leaders surrendered. The British hurriedly tried and executed fifteen leaders. Others, who were imprisoned, lived to become the leaders of a new Ireland.

CHAPTER

FOUR

Two Irelands

54

For a few days in 1916, Ireland had an Irish government. It didn't last, but sympathy for the Irish cause was growing. In 1918, the political party called Sinn Féin (meaning "We Ourselves") won seventy-three seats in Parliament. This party had been founded in 1905 by several organizations favoring separation from England. It gained strength among the many men and women who were imprisoned after the Easter Rising.

Opposite: **A mural shows an Irish Republican Army volunteer.**

Rather than take their seats at the legislature in London, the seventy-two Irish men and one woman established a new Irish legislature, *Dáil Éireann*, meaning "Irish Assembly." The one woman was Countess Markievicz, an English-woman born Constance Gore-Booth. With her election to Parliament, she became the first woman ever to be elected to the House of Commons, though she, too, refused to take her seat. She was in prison at the time— charged with treason for dealing with Germany during the war.

Countess Constance Markievicz

Maud Gonne, Revolutionary and Yeats's Love

Maud Gonne was the daughter of an English officer. On her arrival in Dublin at age seventeen, she met the poet W. B. Yeats, and a famous romance began. She rejected his proposals of marriage but remained the love of his life.

Gonne, avidly interested in the cause of Irish nationalism, was one of the founders of Sinn Féin. Her activities for independence became more public after her husband, Major John MacBride, was executed by the English for his part in the Easter Rising. Gonne herself spent some months in jail in London.

Gonne's son, Sean MacBride, was made chief of staff of the Irish Republican Army. Eventually, he became head of Amnesty International and won the Nobel Peace Prize in 1974.

The New Government

The creation of the Dáil won the support of voters in twenty-six counties, all of which treated this new Irish legislature as if it had every right to be running their not-yet-born nation. The members elected American-born Éamon de Valera as

Michael Collins—The "Big Fellow"

Born near Clonakilty in County Cork in 1890, Michael Collins worked in London. There he joined the Irish Republican Brotherhood. In 1916, he returned to Ireland and began building up an underground army. An important military leader in the Easter Rising of 1916, he was twice imprisoned in Britain.

When the War of Independence broke out in 1919, Collins organized weapons, intelligence, and guerrilla warfare for the Irish Republican Army. He was always in hiding because the British wanted him killed. Once when undercover agents plotted to kill him, he found them first and had them shot. The Black and Tans took revenge and killed fourteen spectators at a hurling game in a park.

Truce was declared between England and Ireland. Collins helped to negotiate the Anglo-Irish Treaty. Though he didn't wholly agree with the treaty, he was put in charge of administering it. Civil war, between those Irishmen who opposed the treaty and those who agreed with it, followed. On August 22, 1922, while inspecting troops, Collins, who was temporarily head of government, was ambushed, probably by fellow Irishmen, at Béal na Bláth in County Cork. The Big Fellow died from a shot in the head and was buried in Dublin.

president. They established a court system, local governments, and a tax system to pay for it all.

The British continued to attempt to administer the whole of Ireland. Members of the Irish Republican Army (IRA) sabotaged those attempts and sometimes attacked Irish people who supported the British. Many of the Irish police resigned rather than try to deal with both sides. The British brought in ex-soldiers to serve as police. Called the Black and Tans for their uniforms, they were hated by the Irish who favored one republican nation. Both sides did terrible things.

A Divided Island

Desperate to stop the fighting, the British parliament passed the Government of Ireland Act, also known as the Anglo-Irish Treaty, which created two Irelands. The six counties of Northern Ireland, which had not supported the Dáil, started functioning almost immediately as a province of the United

Kingdom. Its first legislature was opened by King George V on June 22, 1921.

Members of the Irish Republican Girl Raiders stop an English mail cart.

On the rest of the island, though, a terrible rift grew between those who supported the Anglo-Irish Treaty, and those who refused to accept it. For a year, civil war raged between the factions, with almost 6,000 Irish people killed in the fighting.

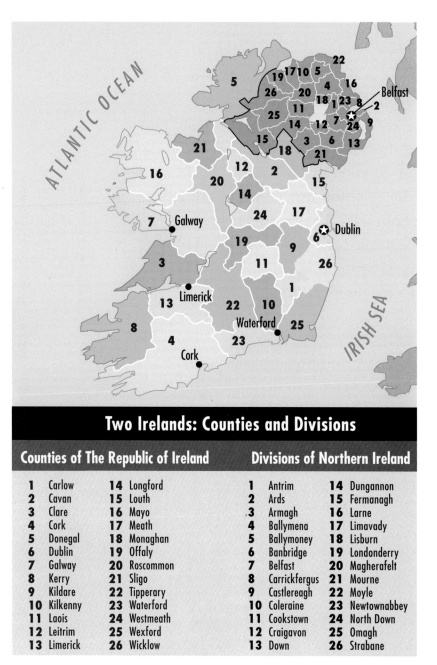

Two Irelands: Counties and Divisions

Counties of The Republic of Ireland

1	Carlow	14	Longford
2	Cavan	15	Louth
3	Clare	16	Mayo
4	Cork	17	Meath
5	Donegal	18	Monaghan
6	Dublin	19	Offaly
7	Galway	20	Roscommon
8	Kerry	21	Sligo
9	Kildare	22	Tipperary
10	Kilkenny	23	Waterford
11	Laois	24	Westmeath
12	Leitrim	25	Wexford
13	Limerick	26	Wicklow

Divisions of Northern Ireland

1	Antrim	14	Dungannon
2	Ards	15	Fermanagh
3	Armagh	16	Larne
4	Ballymena	17	Limavady
5	Ballymoney	18	Lisburn
6	Banbridge	19	Londonderry
7	Belfast	20	Magherafelt
8	Carrickfergus	21	Mourne
9	Castlereagh	22	Moyle
10	Coleraine	23	Newtownabbey
11	Cookstown	24	North Down
12	Craigavon	25	Omagh
13	Down	26	Strabane

At the same time, a new constitution was being written and approved. Éamon de Valera was the new president. He ordered a cease-fire, and in May 1923, most of the Irish reluctantly accepted a divided island.

One of the main reasons for the opposition to the Anglo-Irish Treaty was that it required the Irish to continue to owe allegiance to the British Crown. People elected to the Irish parliament, especially those of Sinn Féin, refused to take the oath of allegiance.

Hoping to soften people's minds, in 1925 de Valera formed a new political party, Fianna Fáil, meaning "Soldiers of Destiny." Those elected from Fianna Fáil finally signed the oath of allegiance by covering up the text when they wrote their names at the bottom. Some members of Sinn Féin and its IRA continued the fight for a unified republic. Their methods were often bloody, and in 1936, the IRA was declared illegal in the Irish Free State.

Éamon de Valera

Born in the United States in 1882 of a Spanish father and Irish mother, Edward de Valera was sent to Limerick as a toddler to live with his grandmother. He became a professor of mathematics, and he joined the Gaelic League, changing his name to the Irish Éamon. Joining the Irish Volunteers, he rose to the rank of captain. His troops fought in the Easter Rising, and he went to prison when the Irish were forced to surrender.

From prison, he was elected president of the Sinn Féin party. When Sinn Féin won its parliamentary victory in 1918, he escaped from prison using a smuggled key. He traveled in secret to the United States, where he gained the support of millions of people of Irish descent and raised money for the treasury of the new Irish Free State.

De Valera refused to support the Anglo-Irish Treaty, and he lost the presidency of the Dáil. However, his new political party, Fianna Fáil, soon controlled the Dáil. De Valera abolished the oath of allegiance to the Crown that had so embittered him. His party also wrote a new constitution that broke ties to the United Kingdom and gave the Irish Free State its new name: Éire, or Ireland.

De Valera was prime minister, or *Taoiseach*, for most of the years from 1932 to 1959. Then, already 77 years old, he was elected president of the Republic of Ireland. He served from 1959 to 1973. He died in 1975.

The 1937 Constitution

By 1937, with the oath of allegiance still a bone of contention, de Valera wrote a new constitution for Ireland. It left out all references to the Crown and the United Kingdom. On July 1, the voters approved the new constitution by 685,105 to 526,945. The twenty-six counties of Ireland had officially become a Gaelic-speaking republic named Éire.

The new constitution made the Republic a Roman Catholic nation and gave the Church a "special position." This meant that it could control marriage, divorce, and family planning, as well as anything else the Church thought important. Many Protestants who hadn't left the country previously did so now. They were alarmed at living in a nation apparently controlled by the pope in Rome. Interestingly, the first president under the new constitution was a Protestant, Douglas Hyde.

Causing problems for the next sixty years was another article in the new constitution. Article 2 said, "The national territory consists of the whole island of Ireland, its islands and the territorial seas."

The Protestants of Northern Ireland were determined to remain part of the United Kingdom. The only way they saw to do that was to keep all Catholics out of public affairs, or even decent jobs. They were successful for thirty years.

World War II

A new war was about to start in Europe. Éire declared that it would be neutral in the event of war. British prime minister Neville Chamberlain agreed that people in Northern Ireland would not be drafted into the British armed services, since the residents of the Republic would not be. However, it's been estimated that at least 50,000 Irish people, in both the north and the south, volunteered to fight for Great Britain.

Irish neutrality in what was called the Emergency did not prevent German bombs meant for England from falling on Ireland. In one attack in 1941, thirty-four people were killed in Dublin. In addition, aircraft from the United States, Canada, Britain, and Germany sometimes crashed in Ireland, killing hundreds. Two deliberate German air raids bombed Belfast, killing or wounding more than a thousand people.

Members of the IRA, which had not disbanded, took the opportunity of wartime commotion to set off bombs in England. Both in England and in Ireland, IRA members were arrested and kept in prison throughout the war.

Growing and Changing

Ireland did not recover quickly from its own past. In the 1950s, unemployment was very high. At least 40,000 people left the country each year. Most went to England. Soon about 15 percent of all people born in Ireland were living elsewhere.

Sean Lemass, who became prime minister in 1959, began a major program to improve the economy of the nation, hoping to keep the Irish in Ireland. Lemass encouraged foreign investment, especially in rural areas. Soon the whole economy improved.

Despite setbacks, Ireland worked on joining the modern world. The European Economic Community, or EEC, was founded in 1957 to help European nations overcome barriers that had slowed their economic development after World War II. Ireland became a member in 1972. The organization (later called the European Union, or EU) started to pour money into its newest member. Ireland was able to improve its ports, roads, and other transportation facilities.

The Troubles Begin

For decades, the Catholics who remained in the North were consistently discriminated against. They couldn't vote without owning land, and they were kept from buying land. They had great difficulty finding jobs. Though they are often identified as Catholics in a Protestant majority, their political stance opposing union with the United Kingdom was more important than their religion.

Starting in the 1960s, the Catholic minority of the North began to agitate for their civil rights. They wanted equality with the Protestants for housing, education, and jobs. The Protestants feared that if the Catholics were not suppressed, Northern Ireland could end up part of the Republic. Catholic civil rights marches were violently attacked.

A paramilitary organization that took the old name of the Irish Republican Army formed to protect the Catholics. Then the British government sent in army troops to preserve order, but they favored the Protestants. Protestant paramilitary groups, calling themselves Loyalists, formed to fight the IRA.

The struggle that would occupy the following decades was building. More than 3,000 people would die in the Troubles.

British soldiers stand guard in Belfast after rioting.

The fighting spread through the neighborhoods of Belfast, Londonderry, and other cities. Walls were put up between neighborhoods occupied by Protestants and by Catholics. Marketplaces became targets for bombings. Car bombs exploded. Sniper fire hit innocent people going about their daily activities.

January 30, 1972, went down in Northern Irish history as Bloody Sunday. The Derry Civil Rights Association was marching to protest the British move to imprison people without trial.

British soldiers fired on the marchers, killing thirteen. Seven of them were teenagers. The British government claimed the soldiers were not to blame. Anger increased. Within days, the British government dissolved the Northern Ireland parliament and took direct control of the province from London.

Though the fighting was about Northern Ireland, the Republic was not free from bloodshed. On what was to be a day of national mourning for the Bloody Sunday massacre, the British embassy in Dublin was burned to the ground. On May 17, 1974, three bombs exploded in downtown Dublin, killing 28 and injuring more than 200.

When the British imprisoned IRA terrorists, they treated them as criminals. Ten men starved themselves to death at Long Kesh (called Maze) Prison near Belfast, hoping to force Britain to classify them as prisoners of war. The first and perhaps the most famous to die was twenty-six-year-old Bobbie Sands, a member of the Northern Ireland parliament. After 66 days of taking in nothing but water and salt, Sands died on May 5, 1981. After nine more men died in the following weeks, the British government agreed to allow the prisoner-of-war status.

Peace Marches and Prizes

In August 1976 in Belfast, British soldiers shot an IRA man who was driving a car. The car went out of control and killed three children. In their outrage, the aunt of the three and another woman who had witnessed the event formed the Community of Peace People. Mairéad Corrigan-Maguire and Betty Williams were determined that, starting with adults and children in the neighborhoods, peace could be brought to Northern Ireland. They organized thousands of Catholics and Protestants, walking together through the devastated parts of Belfast. The two women won the Nobel Prize for Peace in 1976.

The Road to Peace

Despite the violence, the two sides did not stop talking with each other. The United States played an important role in lowering the temperature of the Troubles when President Bill Clinton invited Gerry Adams, president of Sinn Féin in the North, to Washington, D.C. As a result of this international recognition, the IRA called a cease-fire on August 31, 1994. A few weeks later, two Loyalist paramilitary groups joined in.

During the cease-fire, roadblocks were removed from Belfast and other cities. People discovered the pleasures of living without the constant fear of violence. They could walk at night without fear of sniper bullets.

In November 1995, President Clinton became the first sitting American president to visit Northern Ireland. He met with leaders of both sides. Former U.S. senator George Mitchell (who was of Irish descent) was named to lead peace negotiations the following year.

Gerry Adams

A Fresh Start

The negotiations took two years, but on Good Friday of 1998 an agreement was reached. A North-South Council of Ministers was established. The Good Friday Accord was signed on April 10, 1998.

Neither side emerged from the talks with all they wanted. Sinn Féin gave up their insistence that the English get out of

Northern Ireland. In return, the Protestants gave Sinn Féin the right to participate in government. The Republic of Ireland agreed to remove Article 2, which claimed the six counties of Ulster as part of Éire, from its constitution.

Later, the Protestant Unionists refused to hold discussions with Sinn Féin, which they interpreted as backing the Irish Republican Army. It looked as if the agreement might fall apart. But the people of Northern Ireland were tired of the continuing struggle. On May 22, 1998, 81 percent of the people turned out to vote on the Good Friday Accord. About 70 percent of those voting approved the pact. In the Irish Republic, 94 percent registered their approval.

A month later, voters in Northern Ireland again turned out, this time to elect 108 representatives to their new assembly. They made a leap of faith that the IRA would disband and that violence would be a thing of the past.

On August 15, 1998, it once again looked as if the accord would collapse, when a car bomb exploded in a market in Omagh, killing 29 people and injuring 350. It was exploded by a group calling itself the Real IRA, because it disagreed with the IRA's disarmament.

Only months later, David Trimble, leader of the major Protestant political party, and John Hume, leader of the major Catholic political party, were jointly named winners of the 1998 Nobel Peace Prize. The chairman of the Nobel committee said, hopefully, "The vicious circle of violence has been broken."

London returned power over Northern Ireland to the leaders in Belfast on December 2, 1999. Within weeks, though, it looked once again as if the peace would collapse. The British government suspended the assembly. When the different parties reached agreement again, Britain turned the governing of Northern Ireland back to its own assembly on May 29, 2000.

In 2001, hopes rose and fell. First, some Unionists backed away from joint power, fearful that Northern Ireland would be drawn into the Republic. David Trimble, first minister of Northern Ireland, resigned in frustration. Catholic children were attacked on their way to school. Then, just as Britain was about to suspend the assembly again, the IRA began to destroy its weapons. Once again there was hope that the Good Friday Accord would succeed. No one is certain what the future will bring.

When King George V opened the Northern Ireland parliament in 1921, he called for "a day in which the Irish people, North and South, under one Parliament or two, as those Parliaments may themselves decide, shall work together in common love for Ireland."

More than eighty years have passed. But there remains hope that the Irish people will finally work together and that the day King George invoked might come to pass.

David Trimble (left) and John Hume (right) sitting with British prime minister Tony Blair.

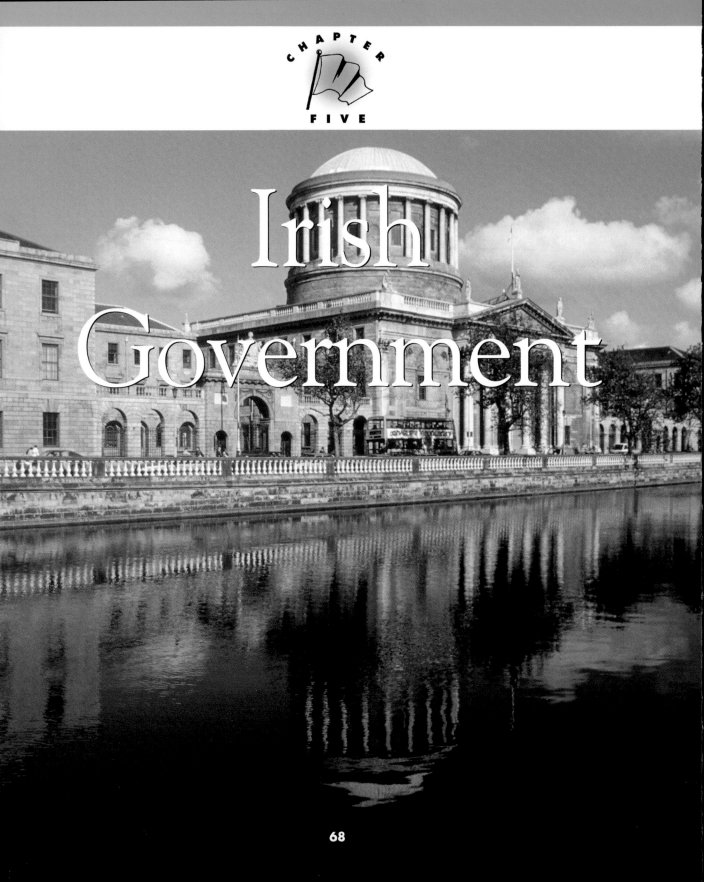

Irish Government

THE REPUBLIC OF IRELAND HAS A WRITTEN CONSTITUTION—
unlike England and thus unlike Northern Ireland—which
functions half on tradition and half on written laws. Passed in
1937, the Republic's constitution made Ireland an independent, sovereign nation. The constitution can be amended, or
changed, by a vote of the people, and it has frequently been
amended. An amendment in 1948 severed all ties with Britain.

In 1995, the people of the Irish Republic voted narrowly
for an amendment in favor of allowing divorce. Ireland was
the last European nation to prohibit divorce.

Opposite: **Four Courts building, where the Supreme Court meets**

Two Flags

The Irish Republic's flag has three vertical bands of color of equal width: green, orange, and white. The green is said to represent the Roman Catholics, the orange is for the Protestants, and the white is for unity. During the Troubles, it was said that the white was keeping the two sides apart.

Northern Ireland's national flag, of course, is the Union Jack, the flag of the United Kingdom. The province's own flag is white with red bands across it in both directions, rather like a Christmas present. A six-pointed star with a red hand on it and gold crown over it is at the crossing point of the bands. This design makes up part of the Union Jack.

Citizens of Ireland are also citizens of the European Union. They are free to move among all the other nations of the EU. The Irish people elect fifteen representatives to the European parliament.

Head of State

Supporters greet President Mary McAleese.

The head of state of the Republic is the president. The president is elected by the people for a period of seven years and can be reelected once. The president does not have any administrative, or executive, power over the government. The president acts on the advice of a fifteen-member cabinet of ministers, which is in the control of the prime minister, or Taoiseach. The prime minister is nominated by the president. The prime minister is usually the head of the party that gains the most seats in the legislature.

If the president dies, a commission takes his or her place. The commission is made up of the chief justice and the leaders of the two houses of parliament.

First Woman President

Mary Bourke Robinson, born in 1944 in Ballina in County Mayo, was Ireland's first female president and thus its first female commander-in-chief. With a law degree from Trinity and after studying further at Harvard University in the United States, she became a professor of law at Trinity. She joined the Labor Party and served in the Irish Senate, or *Seanad*, for many years. As an attorney, she played a leading role in many widely publicized human-rights cases, both in Ireland and in Europe as a whole. She was elected president in 1990 by a considerable margin. She resigned in 1997 to become United Nations high commissioner for human rights. Mary Robinson was followed in office by Mary McAleese.

The Legislature

The two-house legislature, or parliament, is the *Oireachtas*. Members are elected to parliament every five years. The *Oireachtas* meets in Dublin in Leinster House, which was built in 1745.

Leinster House

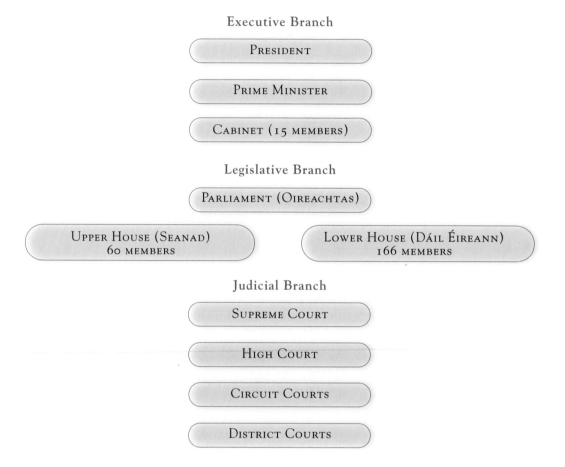

NATIONAL GOVERNMENT OF THE REPUBLIC OF IRELAND

Executive Branch

PRESIDENT

PRIME MINISTER

CABINET (15 MEMBERS)

Legislative Branch

PARLIAMENT (OIREACHTAS)

UPPER HOUSE (SEANAD)
60 MEMBERS

LOWER HOUSE (DÁIL ÉIREANN)
166 MEMBERS

Judicial Branch

SUPREME COURT

HIGH COURT

CIRCUIT COURTS

DISTRICT COURTS

The lower house, or house of representatives, is the Dáil Éireann. The Dáil has 166 members from 41 regions. The number of representatives from each region, or constituency, varies between three and five. The members are *Teachta Dála*, popularly called TDs.

The upper house, or *Seanad*, has sixty members, none of them directly elected by the people. Instead, they are chosen by a variety of groups. Eleven are named by the Taoiseach. Six members are named by the universities, and the remaining forty-three are chosen by people from education, agriculture, labor, industry, and administration.

On the local level, councils administer the counties. They also oversee the governing of many towns within each county. Some larger towns, such as Dublin and Waterford, are governed by independent councils.

The Judicial System

Judges are appointed by the president, on the suggestion of members of the government. Starting at the bottom level, there are twenty-three district courts, with a total of fifty judges. Cases in a district court are tried by a judge without a jury. Any case requiring a jury is sent to the circuit court. There are eight circuits, with twenty-five judges each. Criminal cases in circuit courts are tried with twelve-member juries.

Above that is the high court, which has seventeen judges. When dealing with criminal cases, the high court serves as the central criminal court. The first woman appointed to the high court, in 1980, was Mella Carroll in Dublin.

The top court is the supreme court, consisting of seven judges plus a chief justice. This court is the court of final appeal from lower courts and the judge of the constitutionality of laws being considered by the Dáil.

Dublin: Did You Know This?

The Dublin area, located on the River Liffey, has been the center of Irish trade and industry since it was founded by the Vikings. The name means "black pool." When the Anglo-Normans arrived, they made Dublin their capital. It has continued to grow ever since. During and after the Great Hunger, the population of Ireland shrank drastically, but the number of people in Dublin continued to increase. Today, it has nearly a million people.

Because of the ease with which the Dublin region can be reached by the English, it has always been quite different from the rest of the country. In the seventeenth and eighteenth centuries, it was fashionable for the English to have beautiful city homes in Dublin. These houses deteriorated greatly after the Great Hunger and during the fighting leading up to formation of the Irish Republic. Many of the beautiful squares on which these houses are found turned into slums, and only in recent decades have they been restored to their classic beauty.

Grafton Street connects St. Stephen's Green, a beautiful city park, with Trinity College. Many fancy shops and businesses are located along Grafton Street. Parallel to it is Kildare Street, where Leinster House, the National Museum, and the National Library stand. Nearby is Mansion House, the residence of the Lord Mayor of Dublin. The Dáil Éireann met for the first time in 1919 at Mansion House.

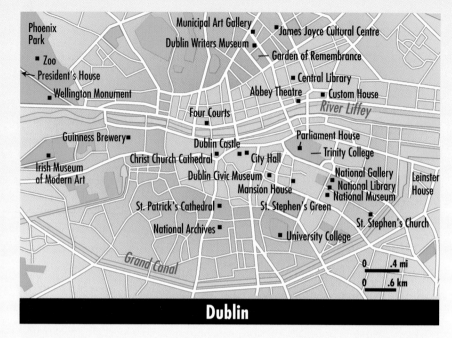

Dublin

West of downtown Dublin is the Phoenix Park, which is the largest fenced park in Europe. The zoo stands at the east end of the park. A tall cross marks the spot where Pope John Paul II held mass in 1979. The official residence of the president of the Republic, called *Áras An Uachtaráin*, is in the park. It looks like the U.S. White House.

Population: 986,000 including surrounding suburbs
Altitude: 223 feet (68 m) above sea level
Average Daily Temperature: 40°F (4°C) in January; 59°F (15°C) in July
Average Annual Rainfall: 30 inches (76 cm)

Sweet Molly Malone

"Molly Malone" is a folk song telling the tale of a Dublin woman who sells cockles and mussels on the streets of Dublin. One of the most photographed sites in Dublin is the statue of Molly Malone on Grafton Street. It was sculpted by Jean Rynhart in 1988.

Northern Ireland

Northern Ireland's status is historically described as a self-governing state (or sometimes province) within the United Kingdom. It was run by the governor, who was elected for six years and who represented the British queen or king. But Northern Ireland hasn't been truly self-governing since 1972. In response to the violence, the British government in London took direct control of Northern Ireland.

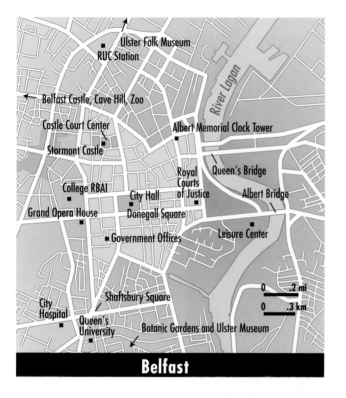

Belfast

During the following years, several attempts were made to start up the province's assembly again, but each failed, until 2000. That's when a new Northern Ireland assembly started with 108 elected representatives. It meets in Stormont Castle outside Belfast, and the government is often popularly referred to as "Stormont."

Northern Ireland elects eighteen members of parliament, or MPs, to represent it in London. It also sends three representatives to the European parliament, which controls the European Union.

The Good Friday Accord calls for a North-South Council of Ministers. This council would have the two countries working together on issues that involve the whole island. Earlier attempts at such a council have failed. Perhaps this one will not.

Belfast is a lovely city, once known the world over for its shipbuilding and linen industries. It has approximately 250,000 residents, having lost more than 40,000 residents in the last twenty years. The central hub of the city is Donegall Square, where City Hall is located. Like Dublin, Belfast has a river—the Lagan—running through it. West of the city is Cave Hill, which contains several man-made prehistoric caves as well as Belfast Castle.

On the opposite side of the city, about 5 miles (8 km) from Donegall Square, is Stormont, where the province's government does its business. Though it looks as if it had been constructed during the eighteenth century, Stormont was built after Partition specifically to house the parliament of Northern Ireland.

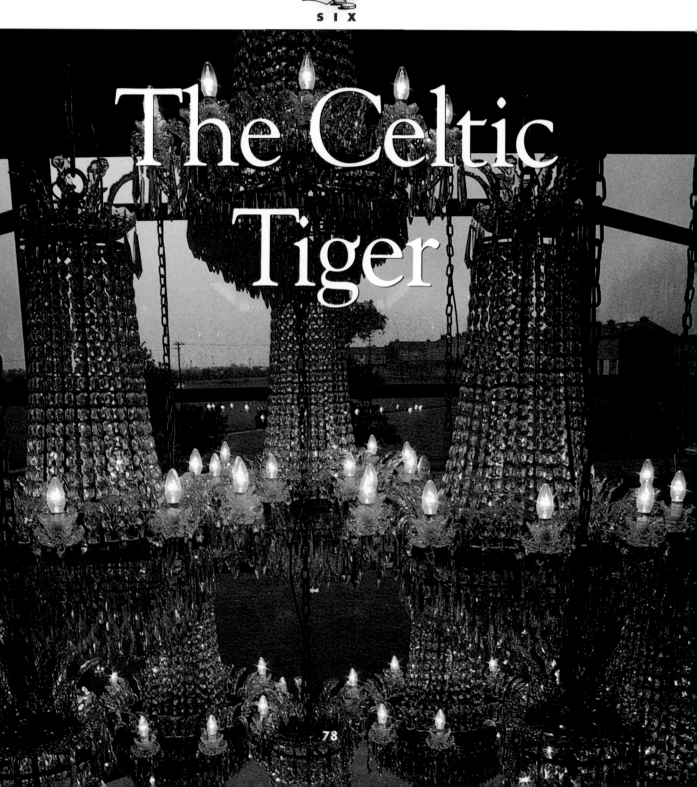

The Celtic Tiger

FOR CENTURIES, IRELAND WAS THE PLACE THAT IRISH CITIZENS left because they couldn't earn a living at home. Devastating underemployment lasted from before the Great Hunger until the 1970s. Millions of Irish men and women took their talents away, helping to build the nations of the United States, Australia, New Zealand, and Canada.

Getting Ready for the Future

By the early 1970s, Ireland was nearly bankrupt. It had been borrowing money for years and could no longer pay its debts. Change began when the government accepted that Ireland had to fix its economy in order to be equal to other nations.

In 1972, Ireland joined the European Economic Community, now called the European Union. It had to agree to stop spending and get its budget in order. Ireland was so poor that it was entitled to huge subsidies (aid payments) from the EU. The Dáil voted to reduce corporate taxes in order to attract foreign companies to make products that would be exported to the European continent.

The plan was progressing when the international recession (slowdown in business) happened in the 1980s. Ireland found itself once again with an unemployment rate of more than 25 percent. Many talented Irish people moved away, mostly to Great Britain and the United States.

New computer companies have made Ireland a great software producer.

Then foreign companies took a good hard look at Ireland. They discovered a well-educated young population crying out to work. Many of the U.S.'s huge computer software and networking firms opened operations in Ireland to supply the European market.

Among the U.S. companies that opened branches in Ireland were Microsoft, Dell, Compaq, and Intel. Today, Ireland's largest employer is the computer industry, and the country manufactures more computers than any other country in the world. Ireland also produces its own software, which is sold globally. Because of its economic growth, Ireland has been called the Celtic Tiger.

Ireland's Money

Until January 1, 2002, the Irish pound, or *punt*, is the Republic of Ireland's legal currency. After that date, the euro, the currency used by countries in the European Union, will be the only legal currency in the Republic. The punt is divided into 100 pence. Punt banknotes come in denominations 5, 10, 20, 50, and 100 punts. There are 1-, 2-, 5-, 10-, 20-, and 50-pence coins, as well as a 1-punt coin. In February 2001, 1 punt equaled U.S. $1.17.

Northern Ireland's currency has the same denominations of banknotes and coins as the Irish punt. However, Northern Ireland's currency is based on the British pound sterling and has the same

value as the British pound. In October 2001, 1 pound equaled U.S. $1.45.

Cathleen ni Houlihan, a character created by poet W. B. Yeats, symbolizes Ireland. She was given permanent form on the Irish Republic's first banknote, issued in 1922. Yeats, who was a senator at the time, suggested in 1926 that animals be used on Irish coins. The 1-punt coin has a well-antlered red deer on it. "Heads" is the side with animals, while "tails" refers to the side with the Irish harp, which appears on all Irish coins. Yeats is one of two famous Irish writers who appear on Irish currency. He is on the 20-punt note, and James Joyce is on the 10-punt note. A special millennium 1-punt coin shows St. Brendan's boat.

Northern Ireland has not been so successful in recent years. Once the Troubles started in Northern Ireland, however, its economy began to deteriorate because few other nations were willing to trade in a place that seemed to always be at war. Most of the industrial plants in Northern Ireland are owned by companies in Great Britain.

Natural Resources

Ireland has little in the way of minerals, but it does have Europe's largest supplies of zinc and lead. The major mines are around Tipperary and Kilkenny.

Small natural gas fields are off the coasts of Ireland. Natural gas is piped from under the sea to Cork, from which it is piped to Dublin. These small fields, however, will not last long, and plans are made to connect Ireland to the British North Sea gas supplies.

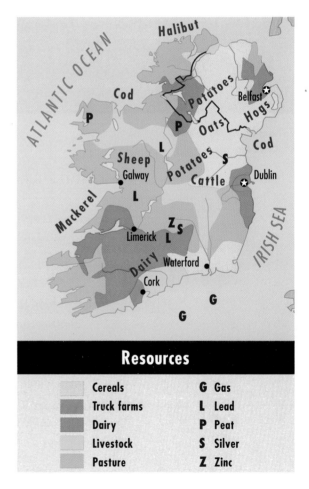

Resources

Cereals	**G** Gas
Truck farms	**L** Lead
Dairy	**P** Peat
Livestock	**S** Silver
Pasture	**Z** Zinc

Fishing boats in the port of Killybegs

Fishing is an important industry for the Republic, with several thousand people earning a living fishing. However, as part of the European Union, Irish fishers are being reduced in number. Much fish is grown now in special farms using aquaculture. At least 80 percent of the salmon that draw tourists to the rivers and streams of Ireland were hatched in fish hatcheries and then released.

What the Republic of Ireland Grows, Makes, and Mines

Agriculture (1999)

Sugar beets	1,712,000 metric tons
Barley	1,278,000 metric tons
Wheat	597,000 metric tons

Manufacturing (1999) *(in Irish pounds)*

Electrical and optical equipment	15,545,000
Chemical products	14,294,000
Food products	11,364,000
Metals and engineering goods	2,424,000

Mining (1997)

Zinc	194,796,000 metric tons
Lead	45,149,000 metric tons
Alumina	1,273,000 metric tons

Manufacturing

At the end of the twentieth century, 39 percent of the Republic's national income came from manufacturing, while only 5 percent was from agriculture. The remainder derived from the service industries, especially tourism.

Unlike many other small nations, Ireland has become fully a part of the global economy. It exports many products to other countries. Computers, software, and pharmaceuticals (medicines) are at the top of the list of items manufactured in Ireland today.

Northern Ireland's manufacturing is part of the United Kingdom's. Some smaller factories producing specialty items are known the world over. Belleek in County Fermanagh, for example, is famous for its pottery, which has a slight pearly translucence to it that is unique. Waterford crystal is another important product. Waterford crystal is made from molten

System of Weights and Measures

The metric system is the official system of weights and measurements in both the Republic of Ireland and Northern Ireland. However, gasoline is measured in imperial gallons, and beer and milk in imperial pints. Imperial measures are larger than U.S. measures. For example, 1 U.S. gallon equals 3.785 liters, but 1 imperial gallon equals 4.546 liters.

A worker etches a piece of Waterford crystal.

glass, etched with elaborate designs, then polished to a sparkle. The United States is the main market for both Belleek pottery and Waterford crystal.

Agriculture

Ireland has always been an island of farmers. Even after the Irish Free State was founded, the government expected Ireland to remain an agricultural nation. The average farm is about 72 acres (29 ha). Farms of such size cannot produce crops in economic quantities. Livestock is more important.

Siblings with lambs on their farm

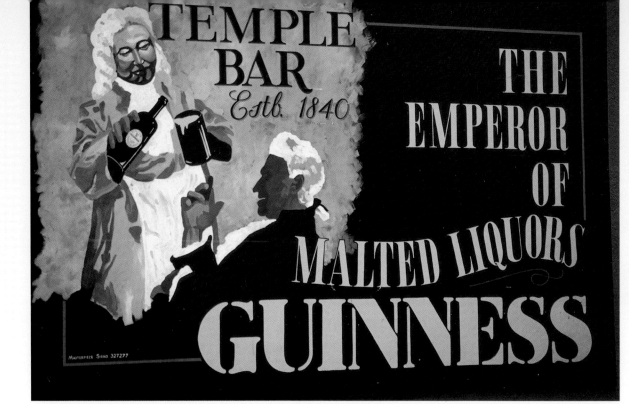

Guinness Stout

For generations, Ireland's most famous manufactured product has been Guinness, a dark, heavy beer. In the twentieth century, it came to be called stout because it was "stouter"—meaning more robust—than other beers. It was created by Arthur Guinness, a native of Celbridge, County Kildare. In 1759, he started a brewery in Dublin, using water from the nearby river.

Guinness went against the tradition of brewing only for local drinkers by using Ireland's barge system to carry his beer to outlying areas. Eventually, the firm became the largest brewery in Europe. Its popularity grew in the United States after *The Guinness Book of Records*, which was created for use in pubs, began to be published internationally.

The main products from agriculture, in order from the most value, are cattle, diary products, noncereal crops, pigs, and sheep and lambs. Grains, especially barley, are used in making beer.

The dairy industry in Ireland leads the world in the use of machinery. Hundreds of cows can be tended and milked with only a few people doing the work.

This store sells a variety of Irish woolens.

For several centuries, the word "linen" had automatically meant Irish linen. The center of the linen industry was in Northern Ireland. It began three hundred years ago when the English encouraged the growing of flax plants for linen to keep Irish woolens from competing with English woolens. Today, Ireland is known for both linen and woolen fabrics. Northern Ireland now produces synthetic textiles.

All Tourists Are Irish

Tourism is Ireland's most important industry. More than a million Americans alone visited Ireland in 2000. An important part of the tourism business is providing shops where tourists can buy Irish goods to take home. Among the major chains of such shops is the Blarney Woollen Mills. Visitors can purchase clothing, CDs of traditional music, crystal, and handcrafted items.

The Republic has put a great deal of effort into reconstructing old places around the country. They know that such places are

Tourists crowd a street in Dublin.

part of the attraction Ireland has for tourists. For example, an old castle at Bunratty near Shannon Airport is used for medieval banquets which are popular with visitors. Many English manor houses have been turned into hotels and inns.

In Touch with the World

Ferry services to Britain go between Dublin and Holyhead in Wales and between Rosslare in County Wexford and Pembroke. One ferry service, Stena Sealink, makes the crossing in ninety minutes in its new high-speed boat. Ferries also carry passengers between Belfast and Stranraer in Scotland and between Belfast and Liverpool in England. France can be reached by ferry to Le Havre from Rosslare.

The main airport in the Republic for transatlantic flights is Shannon. Around it is the Shannon Free Zone, where companies just getting started can set up with many tax benefits as well as help from development experts. Shannon is the headquarters of Aer Lingus, the state-owned airline.

Dublin Airport, also an international airport, is much busier than Shannon. Frequent flights go from Dublin to all of the five airports around London, as well as all over the world. British airlines serve Belfast International Airport.

As the twenty-first century started, Ireland's economy as a whole was growing at an amazing average rate of more than 8 percent per year. Such growth will probably slow down as subsidies from the EU are cut. In addition, Ireland will have to raise its corporate taxes in line with other EU countries. But the roar of the "Celtic tiger" can be heard around the world.

The Irish

I N 2000, AN ESTIMATED 3,797,257 PEOPLE LIVED IN THE
Republic of Ireland. The population density of the Republic is
about 140 people per square mile (54 per sq km), though most
people live in the east and the south.

Opposite: **Irish schoolgirls**

**People on a busy
Dublin street**

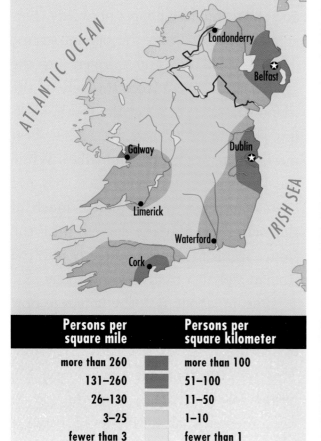

Persons per square mile		Persons per square kilometer
more than 260		more than 100
131–260		51–100
26–130		11–50
3–25		1–10
fewer than 3		fewer than 1

Population of Major Cities (2001)	
Greater Dublin	986,000
Cork	186,400
Limerick	82,000
Galway	59,400
Waterford	45,700
Belfast, Northern Ireland	257,000

Northern Ireland has a population of 1,663,300, which gives it a population density of 305 per square mile (118 per sq km). Northern Ireland has half as many people as the Republic crowded into one-fifth of the land.

Developing the Irish Language

Ogham stone in County Waterford

The first Irish written language is called *ogham*, named for Ogmios, the Celtic god of writing. Its alphabet of twenty characters is known from the ogham stones. These are tall, flat stones driven into the ground at various places throughout the island, though mostly in the south, starting about A.D. 300 to 500. They bear mostly names of people and tribes. While the language carved onto them has not been completely reconstructed, much of the series of notches carved into the stones seems to translate directly into the Roman alphabet that we know today.

Starting about 700, the language now called Old Irish was used. Its alphabet of seventeen letters was based on Latin. This was the language used during the heyday of the High Kings, the period when the heroic classical tales of Irish history were first written down.

Modern Irish began to develop about 1200. It's a mixture of Old Irish, Norse from the Vikings, Norman from the Anglo-Norman invaders, and Middle English. English started being used in Ireland after 1169, when the Anglo-Normans moved in and took over. They brought with them servants from England. While the "bosses" spoke French, the servants spoke English, which gradually the Irish people began to speak, too.

The Irish Language

Irish, or Gaelic, is one of the Celtic languages. Irish, Scottish, and Manx (from the Isle of Man, where it is no longer used) belong to the Gaelic division of Celtic. The other division includes Welsh, Breton (in France), and Cornish (from Cornwall in England, where it is no longer used).

A sign in Gaelic and English

The Irish people themselves call their language *Gaeilge*, meaning Gaelic. But the English mean "Scottish" when they say Gaelic.

The English came close to eliminating Irish from Ireland. Probably fewer than 3 percent of the people use it today as their primary language. The areas where they do are referred to, all together, as the *Gaeltacht*.

As soon as the Irish Free State separated from the United Kingdom in 1921, Irish schools started teaching Irish. The constitution makes Irish the national language and the first official language; English is the second. It wasn't until after World War II that Irish writing was standardized into one form, used in all the schools and official writings. Students graduating from secondary school must pass exams in Irish.

Irish uses only eighteen letters of the alphabet, though the others are used in borrowed words and in science writing. The missing eight letters are j, k, q, v, w, x, y, and z. Some consonants are combined in ways that are not seen in English—bh and dh, for example. Pronunciations are generally different in the Munster counties than elsewhere in the country, but this is changing through the influence of television.

The Celtic Revival

In the late 1800s, it became clear that Irish and Irish culture were endangered. Women of the Ascendancy played an important part in the Celtic Revival, though not many of them actually bothered to learn the Irish language. The Gaelic League was founded in 1893 by Douglas Hyde, a Roscommon

Some Irish Phrases

Conas tá tú?	How are you?
le do thoil	Please
Go raibh maith agat	Thank you
Tá fáilte romhat	You're welcome
Cad is ainm duit?	What's your name?
Éireannaigh	Irish people

Irish Place Names

The same words are used as part of many different place names. They tell something about where the place is located or what place is being named. These are just a few of them in English:

bally	town or townland
cashel	castle
beg	small
dun	fort
kill	church
mor	big
ros	wood or peninsula
bel or *bal*	mouth of a river or valley
ban or *bane*	white
dubh	black

lawyer who was later the first president of the Republic. He had helped to establish the first Irish-language periodical, *Gaelic Union Journal*. The league was founded to promote Irish language, culture, and games.

The People

More than 55 percent of the people of the Republic of Ireland are under the age of twenty-four, and 21 percent are under the age of fifteen. However, the birth rate is dropping rapidly, and the larger part of the population will soon be into their middle years. In 1993, the birth rate dropped below the number needed to replace parents for the first time in Irish history. Life expectancy is seventy-seven years.

Popularly, the Irish are thought to be red-haired and freckled, but only a small portion of the population has these features. An Irish person is just as likely to have dark hair and pale skin. There is a strong streak of Hispanic-looking features among the Irish, perhaps from the sailors of the Spanish Armada. There are also characteristics that derive from Danish, Norman, and English ancestors.

A farmer and his six children

About 10,000 gypsies live in Ireland. Formerly known as tinkers, today they are called the Traveler Community. About half of them are originally Irish—people who were dispossessed

"1" />

"caption"

A Traveler family with their caravan

The Isles of Aran

The three islands called Aran were inhabited for centuries by fishing families. Each family created a distinctive pattern used in knitting sweaters for the members of the family. This wasn't just a craft. It was so that a dead body could be identified if a man were lost off a boat in a storm and later washed ashore. Aran sweaters are popular with knitters the world over.

by the English. The other half are Romany, the ancestral gypsy people of Europe. They are often seen living by the side of the roads in small caravans. They belong to no community but their own.

Moving In

Thousands of Irish people who thought they were leaving Ireland for good when they emigrated are returning to some of the many new jobs available. However, they are stunned by the huge changes that have occurred since they left. Some of them think that Ireland has now become "more American than America." When they left Ireland, they knew things would be different in their new homes. But when they returned, they thought they would find exactly what they had left.

One of the reasons for the change is that newcomers are arriving in Ireland in large numbers. People from other countries have sought asylum in Ireland. In the 1990s, the largest number were from Romania. The nation was building special housing for people seeking political asylum to live in while their cases moved through the courts. Because of Ireland's need for workers, the process was being speeded up as the twenty-first century started.

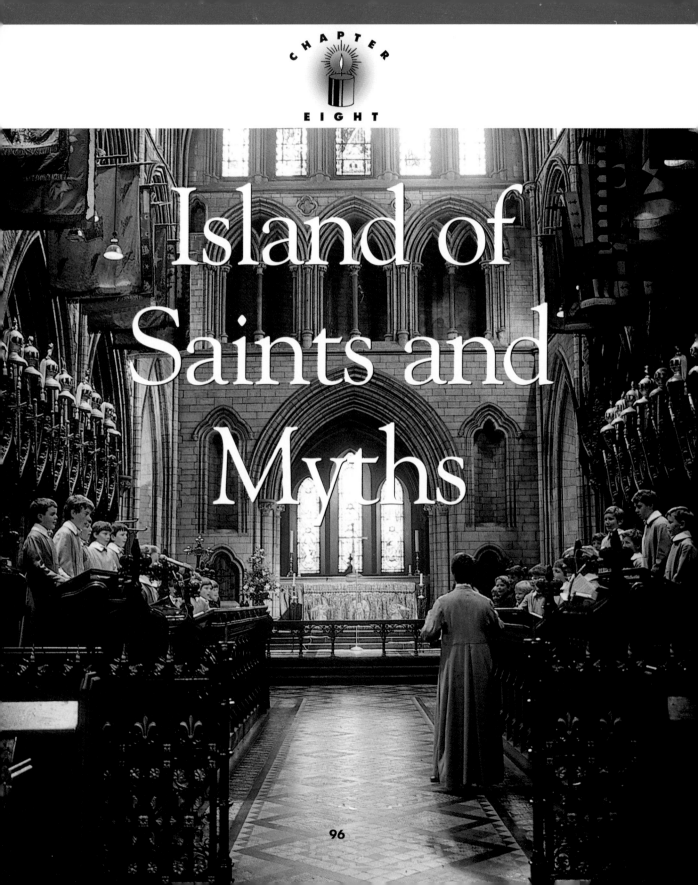

Island of Saints and Myths

THE CELTS OF EARLY IRELAND TOLD TALES THAT ENLIVENED long evenings by the fires. Some of the earliest Irish myths make a woman responsible for founding Ireland. A woman named Banba held a mountaintop in Ireland while Noah's flood raged around her. Among the earliest peoples to appear in the ancient tales are the Tuatha Dé Danann, which means the "Peoples of the Goddess Dann."

Opposite: **St. Patrick's Cathedral choir in Dublin**

The Faerie Folk

Many civilizations have had magical humanlike figures in their mythology. Sometimes referred to as "the good people" or "the little people," fairies (or faeries) of Ireland provide

The Ancient Tales

Some tales involve the hero Cúchulainn, the nephew of the king of Ulster. Cúchulainn's name means "hound of Culann." He gained the name when he slew a particularly ferocious hound—"cu"—belonging to Culann. His main enemy was Maeve, the queen of neighboring Connacht. She was described as amazingly beautiful and able to run faster than any horse.

The sagas of the competition between Cúchulainn and Queen Maeve probably stem from actual conflicts between the chieftains of Ulster and Connacht. Small incidents were retold and retold, taking on heroic features, until eventually they were written down by the monks in early Christian Ireland.

The primary tale about the two concerns a cattle raid. Maeve leads her troops into battle to kidnap a famous bull, which she wants to mate with the white-horned bull owned by her husband, Ailill. Cúchulainn wins the battle, but Maeve manages to get the bull anyway.

Tales of Cúchulainn are called the Ulster Cycle. There are also tales of another hero, Fionn MacCumhaill (or Finn MacCool), called the Fenian Cycle. Supposedly descended from the Druids, Finn is a nature-loving giant whose exploits were very popular in medieval tales. Supposedly, he built the amazing rocks called the Giant's Causeway.

many images we have of these magical creatures. Supposedly, fairies live in *Tír na n-Óg* ("Land of Youth"), which is parallel to our world but invisible to humans. Fairy actions, pleasant and evil, can affect human lives. Finding a four-leaf clover prevents bad fairy-caused things from happening.

Fairies, both male and female, are generally regarded as quite beautiful. They may come from tales of the Tuatha, who were driven underground by the Milesians, the ancestors of humans. Unlike lovely fairies, who live in communities, ugly leprechauns live in ill-tempered isolation.

A sign in County Kerry

Tradition holds that sometimes fairies substitute a fairy infant for a human infant. Such a child is called a changeling. In times past, mentally ill people were often thought of as changelings.

Banshees, or female spirits, supposedly make a terrifying wailing sound that warns when someone is going to die. Contemporary ghost stories often make banshees actually cause the death, but that's not part of Irish tradition.

Religions in the Republic of Ireland		Religions in Northern Ireland	
Roman Catholic	95.0%	Roman Catholic	40%
Protestant	3.4%	Presbyterian	21%
Jewish	0.1%	Church of Ireland	18%
Other	1.5%	Other	12%

The Coming of Christianity

The lad who became the famed saint of Ireland probably grew up near the west coast of Britain. He became a follower of the new faith, Christianity, which had been brought to Great Britain in the early 300s. As a young man, Patrick was kidnapped by invaders from the sea who took him to Ireland as a slave. He spent six years there. He escaped but voluntarily returned to the Celtic island to bring Christianity to the nonbelievers there.

St. Patrick is not the only patron saint of Ireland. St. Columba (also known as St. Columcille), born in 521, might have become a king. Instead, he became a monk and was later recognized as a saint. He founded many monasteries throughout Ireland and, legend says, copied at least 300 books by his own hand. After his death in 597, he became one of Ireland's three patron saints.

The third patron saint is St. Brigid (or Brigit). She and six other women founded the first convent in Ireland. Called Church of the Oaks, it later gave its Irish name to the town that built up around it—Kildare. Brigid was the head of the convent, or abbess, until her death in about 528. Known for her kindness, she worked miracles during her lifetime. St. Brigid's Day is February 1, the beginning of spring.

Symbols of Ireland

The Druid priests of the Celts had used a circular symbol to indicate the sun, which they worshiped. Patrick persuaded the High King to change his circular symbol by combining it with Patrick's symbol, the cross. Together these symbols make up the famed Celtic, or high, cross. The Celtic cross has become—along with the harp and the shamrock—one of the symbols of Ireland.

The Rock of Cashel in Tipperary was the seat of the kings of Munster. This hill is said to be where Patrick explained the Trinity (belief that God is the Father, the Son, and the Spirit) through the three-leaved clover, which is now called the shamrock. The word "shamrock" is the English version of the Irish *seámróg*, meaning "clover."

The Golden Age

Most Irish people were converted to Christianity through the efforts of these early saints. The new Christians often banded together to carry out religious acts, learning, and prayer beyond those expected of the average person. Many of them separated themselves from regular society by living in special places called monasteries, if they were for men (monks), and convents, if they were for women (nuns).

Some monks became hermits, living alone in *clochans*, or beehive houses. These were small, round houses built of layer upon layer of flat stones, gradually closing in on a narrow opening that allowed smoke out. Some of these ancient beehive houses can still be seen.

Beehive house in County Kerry

Clonmacnoise Abbey was a center of medieval learning.

A legend says that St. Patrick's Cathedral was built on the spot where he preached.

The Golden Age of Irish Christianity lasted from the sixth to the ninth centuries. It was the period of great monasteries, such as Clonmacnoise in County Offaly, founded in A.D. 545 by one of the Saints Kieran (there were two). Monasteries became the centers of community, social, intellectual, legal, and religious life. Missionaries went out from Irish monasteries to the Continent, where they were so revered that Ireland became known as "the island of saints." Much of the rest of Europe was going through the period that has been called the Dark Ages, but learning was being preserved in Ireland.

Armagh

St. Patrick himself chose Armagh, in County Armagh, as the center of Irish Christianity, and he built his first stone church there. Though in Northern Ireland, it is still the headquarters of the Irish Catholic Church. Patrick was buried at Downpatrick in

The Book of Kells

The most famous handmade book from the Golden Age is *The Book of Kells*. Though probably created on Iona, it was kept at the monastery in the County Meath town of Kells until it was moved to Dublin for display at Trinity College. It has become one of the most important visits tourists to Ireland make. The town of Kells is asking the university to give its famed book back. Kells has built a visitors' center that shows the monastic life in Kells, and it guarantees that the priceless book would be protected.

County Down—ironically, the grave considered his own is in the Church of Ireland (Protestant) cemetery. The church Patrick built in Armagh is now a Church of Ireland cathedral.

The Archbishop of Armagh is the Primate of All Ireland. The organization of the Catholic Church in Ireland has not changed in nine hundred years, and the different geographic areas of the church, called dioceses, do not reflect today's counties or other divisions.

Centuries of Change

After the Irish saw the Vikings making raids on monasteries, apparently without any punishment from God, they themselves began to try to steal treasure from the great religious houses. The respect with which religious people had been held deteriorated.

After King Henry VIII of England outlawed monasteries in the 1500s, many monks, especially Franciscan friars, donned plain clothing and lived among the people. Teaching in secret, they kept Catholicism alive. But it was difficult to be a Catholic in Ireland.

Important Religious Holidays

St. Patrick's Day	March 17
Easter Sunday	March or April
Feast of the Assumption, Northern Ireland	August 15
Christmas	December 25

In the early seventeenth century, England required that all Irish people in public office take an oath avowing that the monarch was superior to the pope, leader of the Catholic Church. Before the requirement was dropped, seventeen men and women were executed for refusing to take the oath. In the 1990s, all seventeen were beatified. This is a step on the way to sainthood in the Roman Catholic Church.

Today's Churches

Éamon de Valera's view in 1922 of Ireland as a Catholic nation primarily held true. Thirty years later, Labor Party leader Brendan Corish said in a speech, "I am an Irishman second; I am a Catholic first."

Article 8 of the 1922 constitution said, "Freedom of conscience and the free profession and practice of religion" are "subject...to morality." The question of who would determine "morality" was not decided until the constitution of 1937, when the decision was put firmly in the hands of the Roman

Catholic Church. Divorce was outlawed. Schools became Catholic. Discrimination based on religion occurred. Marriage between Catholics and non-Catholics was outlawed.

Many Protestants who might have liked to move to the Republic decided they could not. In 1972, the phrase granting the Roman Catholic Church a "special position" in Ireland was removed from the constitution.

The island as a whole is about 75 percent Catholic, with more than two-thirds of them living in the Republic. About 15 percent of the whole island is Protestant, with more than two-thirds of them living in Northern Ireland. Most of the Protestants belong to the Church of Ireland, which is part of the Anglican Communion, deriving from the Church of England. Many people of Scottish descent are Presbyterians, and many of English descent are Methodists.

Christ Church Cathedral, the oldest church in Dublin

There is a small Jewish community, most of whom live in Dublin, that has existed in Ireland for hundreds of years. There are several Islamic mosques in Ireland. About 10 percent of the people acknowledge no religion.

Words, Music, and Sports

EVEN THE ENGLISH COULDN'T SUPPRESS THE CREATIVITY of the Irish. For centuries, it has flowed primarily into literature and music. Edmund Spenser is only one of many writers associated with Ireland. He colonized an estate in Munster for the English during the 1590s. He wrote the long poem *The Faerie Queen*, often thought to be the greatest poem ever written in English.

Jonathan Swift, whose real name was Isaac Bickerstaff, was born in Dublin in 1667. An Anglican priest, he was dean of Dublin's St. Patrick's Cathedral when he published his satiric novel, *Gulliver's Travels*.

Oliver Goldsmith was born in Pallas, County Longford, in 1728. He is most famous for the novel *The Vicar of Wakefield*, published in 1766, and the play *She Stoops to Conquer*, which is still performed today.

English-born Maria Edgeworth lived at Edgeworthstown in County Longford from 1782 until her death in 1849. She ran her father's estate and became one of the first female

Ireland's Nobel Prizes in Literature

1923	W. B. Yeats, poet and playwright	
1925	George Bernard Shaw, playwright	
1969	Samuel Beckett, playwright	
1995	Seamus Heaney, poet	

The Limerick

English humorist and poet Edward Lear popularized the nonsense poem called the limerick in his 1846 book, *Book of Nonsense*. A limerick is a five-line poem that often starts, "There was a . . .." The first, second, and fifth lines rhyme, and the third and fourth lines, much shorter, also rhyme. This poetry form was supposedly invented by a pub-keeper in Dublin to amuse his customers, though it's not known why it's called a limerick. Perhaps the pub-keeper was from Limerick.

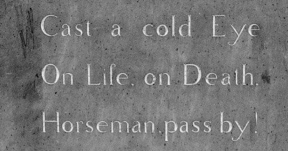

The Sligo Poet

William Butler Yeats lived in cities much of his writing life, but his poetry reflects his youthful years in the northwestern counties of Sligo, Galway, and Donegal. This region is often called Yeats Country. Yeats served as a senator in the new Republic and won the Nobel Prize for Literature in 1923. He died in 1939 and is buried at Drumcliffe in County Sligo. On his tombstone is the mysterious epitaph that he wrote himself, which has puzzled people since his death: "Cast a cold eye on life, on death, Horseman pass by!"

professional writers. Although she wrote several books about Irish life, she was most famous for suspenseful, dramatic novels such as *Castle Rackrent*.

Poet and playwright Oscar Wilde was born in Dublin and educated at both Trinity College and Oxford University. In both places, he became known for his wit and general eccentricity. His only novel, *The Picture of Dorian Gray*, published

The Dublin Joyce

Leopold Bloom, one of the most famous names of Ireland, never existed. He is the lead character in James Joyce's novel *Ulysses*. Joyce was born in Dublin in 1882 and was educated at University College. His first publications were short stories that were later collected as *The Dubliners*. While living in Zurich, he wrote *A Portrait of the Artist as a Young Man*.

He commemorated the date on which he met his love, Nora Barnacle—June 16—in *Ulysses*. The entire long novel takes place on that one day, but it took him many years to write. *Ulysses* is a very complex novel that portrays the characters' thoughts in all their jumbled, random patterns.

Joyce never returned to Ireland after leaving it in 1912. But even his last novel, *Finnegans Wake*, published in 1939, takes place in Dublin. Joyce died in Switzerland two years after the book was published.

The Fantasy Master

C. S. Lewis, a native of Belfast, was a writer who turned out numerous books on the Christian faith. A professor at both Oxford and Cambridge universities in England, he wrote a trilogy of science fiction novels and then published his seven books of fantasy, now called The Chronicles of Narnia. The first one, *The Lion, the Witch, and the Wardrobe*, was published in 1950. His autobiography was called *Surprised by Joy*.

The Vampire and the Actor

The whole world knows Dublin-born Bram Stoker—at least they know his fictional creation Count Dracula. Trained as a civil servant, Stoker loved writing and theater, and he found a position as secretary to the great English actor Sir Henry Irving. The actor and his Lyceum Theatre in London kept Stoker very busy, but he found time to do his own writing. *Dracula* was published in 1897 and was probably based on a vampire novel by another Irishman, Sheridan Le Fanu. The personality of Count Dracula is said to resemble that of Stoker's boss, Sir Henry.

in 1891, is about a man who does not change as he ages, but his portrait turns evil and ugly, reflecting his reality. Wilde was best known for his plays, such as *The Importance of Being Earnest* and *Lady Windermere's Fan*.

More recently, Patrick Kavanagh, author of *Tarry Flynn*, was a popular novelist and poet who lived most of his life near Inniskeen in County Monaghan. He resided in Dublin in the years before his death in 1967.

Irish Theater

The center of the rebirth of Irish culture at the start of the twentieth century was the Abbey Theatre, developed by poet W. B. Yeats and Lady Isabella Augusta Gregory. Already involved in the Irish Literary Theatre, they converted an old morgue on Abbey Street in Dublin into a theater in 1904. The building burned down in 1951, and a new theater was built in its place.

During its first years, the Abbey produced plays based on Celtic mythology. Poet Padraic Colum was responsible for changing the emphasis to naturalism, or rural reality. The biggest name in such realism of life in Ireland was Dublin-born playwright Sean O'Casey (originally John Casey). His two most famous plays, which first appeared at the Abbey and are still being produced, are *Juno and the Paycock*, written in 1924, and *The Plough and the Stars*, from 1926.

The Abbey Theatre Company introduced American audiences to Irish drama by touring with J. M. Synge's now-famous plays *The Playboy of the Western World* and *Riders to the Sea*.

Today, Brian Friel, a native of County Tyrone, has had most of his plays produced first by the Abbey Theatre. Several were produced on Broadway in New York City, and *Dancing at Lughnasa* became an award-winning film.

Traditional Music

Queen Elizabeth I outlawed Irish music in Ireland. She ordered all the people's instruments destroyed and had anyone singing their folk songs arrested. Obviously it didn't work. Today, traditional music is popular worldwide.

Musicians on a Dublin street

The rhythmic accompaniment to traditional (or "trad") Irish music is a one-sided goatskin drum called a *bodhrán*, which means "deafener." Many sounds can be achieved on this drum depending on the way the player uses one hand to strike the skin and the other to vary the tension on it. The melody comes from harps, fiddles (violins held any way that the fiddler

The harp dates back to the time of the Celts.

wants), flutes, and uilleann pipes (the Irish version of bagpipes).

The harp was an Irish instrument from the time of the Celts. The harps we see in symphony orchestras today have a straight column, called a pillar. The Irish harp pillar is curved. The Irish harp is small enough to hold on a lap while being played.

Harpers were important people in the community, for they retold in song the stories of great deeds of the people. Despite the efforts of the English to eliminate harpers, these musicians remained important until at least the sixteenth century. At that time, the Catholic landowning class, which had supported the harpers, died out. Turlough O'Carolan, a blind musician and composer who lived from 1670 to 1738, has been called "the last of the harpers."

The Singers

The Irish tell tales in their songs, called ballads. Most Irish ballads are sad, but not for romantic reasons. Instead, they tell of the long centuries of suppression and oppression. "Bold Robert Emmet, the Darling of Ireland," for example, tells of a real man who fought a lost cause in trying to create an uprising in 1803.

An "Irish tenor" is a singer with a clear, high voice that can sound dramatic and lyrical, especially singing Irish ballads. The most famous Irish tenor during the first half of the twentieth century was Athlone-born John McCormack. At seventeen, he won the Gold Medal at Feis Ceoil, Ireland's annual classical music competition, held in Dublin each year. He became a star in Italian opera, but it was his concerts sung throughout the world that made him popular.

The most famous Irish tenor today is Ronan Tynan, who is a disabled doctor. In 2000, the Kilkenny native gave up his medical practice to tour the world performing. "My heart says for me to sing," he says.

Bringing Back the Music

Seán O'Riada, born John Reidy in Cork in 1931, was instrumental in popularizing traditional Irish music. One group he founded became the core of the Chieftains, a group formed in 1963 by Paddy Moloney. A piper, Moloney had been asked by Claddagh Records to assemble a group of traditional performers. The Chieftains have been playing ever since in concerts around the world. The Clancy Brothers and the Dubliners are also famous recording groups of semitraditional music.

The Chieftains

Bono, lead singer of U2

Less traditional but very popular are recent Irish recording artists such as the group U2, whose lead singer is Bono—real name Paul Hewson—a native of Ballymun, Dublin. The Grammy-winning group performed in the Live Aid concert assembled by Bob Geldof to help feed the starving people of Africa.

Grammy-winner Enya was born in Donegal in 1961. She came from a musical family and was initially a classical pianist. Her first album, recorded in 1986, is called *The Celts*. Dublin-born Sinéad O'Connor both composes and sings her own songs. The group called The Cranberries was started in Limerick. It features three instrumentalists and vocalist Dolores O'Riordan. The movie

The Cranberries

called *The Commitments* is about a band in Dublin, but the band is fictional.

The Dancers

Traditional Irish dancing, called step dancing, never died out in Ireland, but the rest of the world did not know much about it until the 1990s. The dancers hold their upper bodies still while their feet move with amazing speed in intricate and high steps. It has some characteristics of ballet and some of American tap dancing.

Michael Flatley performs "The Lord of the Dance."

In 1994, a group of Irish dancers, led by Bill Whelan and Moya Doherty, put together a short performance of step dancing to be telecast during a Eurovision (European television) broadcast. People found the Irish dancing very exciting, and the dancers decided to turn the brief performance into a full show, which was put on in Dublin. The popularity of the show, called *Riverdance*, spread, and its fans quickly embraced things Irish. It has been responsible for a huge increase in tourism in Ireland.

Irish Sports

The soccer team from the Republic qualified for the World Cup in 1990 and 1994, an unusual feat for such a small country. But the bigger following at home is devoted to Gaelic football. This is a rugged game with fifteen men to a side.

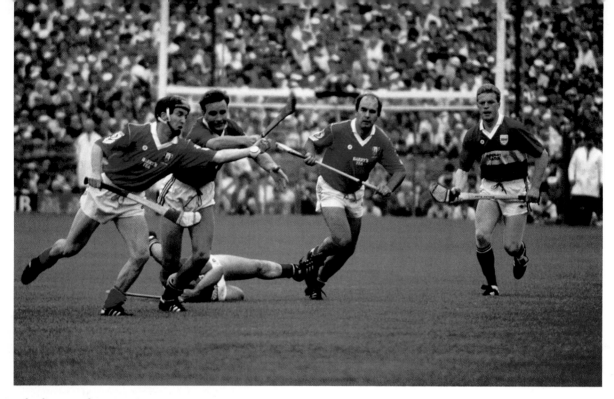

A hurling match

They have to move the ball to the goal in any way they can except throwing it. It has to be dribbled or kicked at least every four steps. A ball that goes below the bar on the goal earns three points, while one above earns only one.

Gaelic football used to be played by the men of many communities, with violent competitions between towns. In 1884, the Gaelic Athletic Association (GAA) was formed to firm up the rules and tone down the violence. They organized the first national championships a few years later. Today, the different teams vie for the All-Ireland Cup.

As peculiarly Irish as Gaelic football is hurling. Using ashwood sticks called hurleys, the fifteen players to a side have to move a small leather ball down the field. It looks rather like a very fast combination of hockey and soccer. Hurling is a very ancient sport that is like a cross between hockey and lacrosse.

A woman's version is called *camogie*. Hurling, like Gaelic football, was revived and organized by the GAA. It is not a professional game.

Irish Horses

Horse racing began in Ireland during the early years of the Celts, who raced horses that resembled today's Arabians on the plains of Curragh, in County Kildare. The area is still known for racing. The Irish Grand National is the big steeplechase (racing over fences) event of the year. The Irish Derby is the big flat race (around a track) of the year.

Competition at the Dublin Horse Show

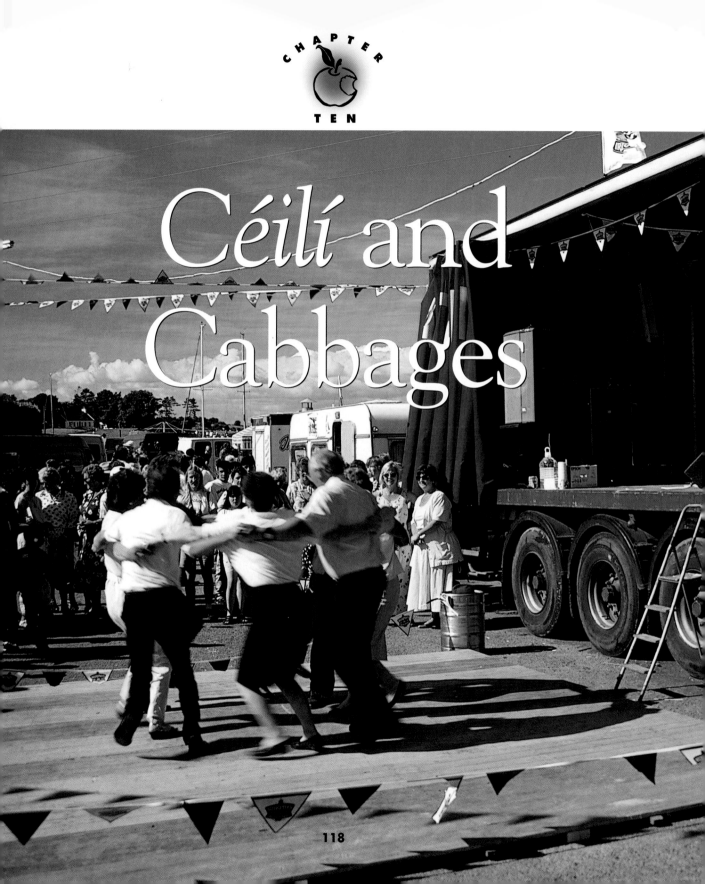

Céili and Cabbages

A SPECIAL EVENT IN THE LIVES OF MANY COUNTRY Irish people is the *céilí* (pronounced KAY-lee), which is a Gaelic term for "neighborly visit." For centuries, the only entertainment that country people had was that which they created themselves. Céilís were gatherings where they would sing, play their instruments, tell stories, and dance.

Such dances came close to dying out in Ireland itself, when the English regarded them as "too Irish." The songs and dances were kept alive elsewhere in the world until it was safe for them to be performed again in Ireland.

Opposite: **A céilí with music and dance.**

Public Holidays in Republic of Ireland (RI) and Northern Ireland (NI)	
New Years's Day	January 1
St. Patrick's Day	March 17
Good Friday	Friday before Easter
Easter Monday	Monday after Easter
May Day	First Monday in May
Spring Bank Holiday (NI)	Last Monday in May
Spring Bank Holiday (RI)	First Monday in June
Orangeman's Day (NI)	July 12
Summer Bank Holiday (RI)	First Monday in August
Summer Bank Holiday (NI)	Last Monday in August
Autumn Bank Holiday	Last Monday in October
Christmas Day	December 25
St. Stephen's Day (RI)	December 26
Boxing Day (NI)	December 26

"Neighborly visits" now take place primarily in pubs, or public houses, which are the center of social life in most small towns. Pubs are not strictly places for adult drinking. In fact, many adults don't drink alcoholic beverages at all. Instead, pubs are the social centers of towns, where entire families gather for singing, dancing, and a good *craic*, or chat.

Education

The Penal Laws that prevented the Irish from practicing their Roman Catholic faith also kept them from educating their young people. During the 1700s, education was kept alive in Ireland at hedge schools. These were classes, held illegally, wherever they could be safe from English troops. Often classes were held outside, which gave these schools their name.

Until 1967, the Irish government was so poor that all parents had to pay large fees to keep their children in school after the age of fourteen. Most Irish young people left school long before they had a decent education. That year, though, the Dáil voted to cancel those fees and make education free to all. Now most children graduate from secondary school.

The Irish Educator

Most Irish boys since the early 1800s have been educated by the laymen (non-priests) of the Congregation of the Brothers of the Christian Schools of Ireland, called simply the Christian Brothers. Edmund Ignatius Rice of Waterford was a ship's supplier who began the Irish Christian Brothers in 1802 to educate the poor boys of Ireland after English laws had failed to educate Irish youth for the future. Rice began his first school in a stable in Waterford. By 1808, when his schools were already spreading, Rice and his fellow teachers took religious vows, creating the religious order that continues the work today. Girls were taught by nuns in local convents.

All children are required by law to go to school from ages six to fifteen. First-level schools are for children from ages six to twelve, such as grade school. Second-level schools teach young people from ages twelve to seventeen. Students who do well in the second-level schools can usually win full scholarships covering university-level education. At least 40 percent go on to university.

Second-level school girls

Education is closely tied to religion, and many of the main events in a child's life are religious in nature. First communion, for example, is recognized as a special event for seven- and eight-year-olds. Girls dress in fancy white dresses and boys in suits. In Northern Ireland, Catholics generally attend church-related schools while everyone else attends public or non-Catholic private schools.

First communion is a special occasion.

The Republic has four universities. The University of Dublin is better known as Trinity College (the original plans called for several colleges within a university, but it didn't happen). The National University of Ireland has campuses in Dublin, Cork, Galway, and Maynooth. Limerick has an independent university founded in 1970. Dublin City University was founded five years later.

Students at Trinity College

Trinity College was established in 1592 for Anglicans only. No one but members of the Church of Ireland was allowed to attend until 1793. Even after that, Catholics weren't allowed to attend without special permission from the Catholic Church. Since 1970, however, there have been many Catholics in the student body.

Northern Ireland has Queen's University, which was founded in Belfast in 1845. The University of Ulster was created in 1984 out of two technical schools. With headquarters at Coleraine, it has campuses at Belfast, Jordanstown, and Londonderry.

Irish Foods

Foods that are particularly Irish are the foods of the poor. Soda bread, called *fadge*, is a round loaf that is cooked with either white flour or whole wheat and with baking soda instead of yeast to lighten it. When raisins are added to white soda bread, the result is called *spotted dog*.

Today, tourists love what is called an Irish breakfast, which probably no poor Irishman would ever have been able to eat. It includes bacon (which is more like American ham than American bacon), sausage, black pudding (a delicious sausage made of oatmeal moistened with pig's blood), eggs, soda bread, tomatoes,

An Irish feast

juice, and tea or coffee. The Irish drink more tea than any other European people, even more than the English.

Corned Beef and Cabbage

The national holiday in the Republic is St. Patrick's Day, March 17. Both the celebration itself and the corned beef (which is beef soaked for a long time in many spices to preserve it) and cabbage associated with the day are recent developments, more popular in the United States than in Ireland. Beef itself does not have a long history in Ireland, because cattle were kept for their dairy products, not their meat.

Cabbage, though, has long been—and is still—Ireland's most popular green vegetable. Historically, it was important because, like potatoes, it could be preserved over the winter. A popular traditional dish called *colcannon* uses both cabbage and potatoes.

Lamb (from a young sheep) or mutton (from an older sheep) is eaten more often than beef. Mutton is the backbone of the ever-popular Irish stew.

The potato has been a basic part of the Irish diet since it was introduced into Ireland by Sir Walter Raleigh, who discovered it in South America. It's been estimated that the Irish eat 40 percent more potatoes than any other European people. Potatoes are served in many ways, though most frequently with butter. Because of Ireland's large dairy industry, butter is still an important item in the daily diet. *Boxty* are pancakes made of shredded potatoes, with all moisture drained out, and fried in butter.

People stroll through a Dublin neighborhood.

Traveling Around

The Irish are walkers, and casual strolls into the city center in the evenings—often with a pub as the destination—are a regular part of family life. In recent years, many of the larger towns have removed automotive traffic from the city centers and made the entire areas around shops and hotels into pedestrian walkways.

A basic form of transportation in Ireland for centuries has been the jaunting car, a small backless cart pulled by a single horse. They are driven by drivers known as *jarveys*. While many other such primitive forms of transport have disappeared, these pony carts continue to be popular with tourists.

Ireland is so small that no place is much more than three hours from Dublin. Public transportation began in Ireland in 1815 with a coach system developed by Italian-born Charles Bianconi. He started with a service between Clonmel and Cahir.

Ireland today has an excellent public transportation system, both throughout the countryside and in Dublin. Irish Rail runs the trains that go out into the countryside and DART, the Dublin Area Rapid Transit system.

Many of the streets in cities were laid out before automobiles existed. Now, with the improving economy, many people own cars. Traffic jams are becoming a feature of the day, especially in Dublin and Belfast.

DART trains whisk people to and from Dublin.

Most Irish people live in or near Dublin, and yet most Irish people continue to feel a kinship with villages and country-side. The Irish use a great deal of color on their houses, delighting the eye and enliving the towns, especially around Dingle. Front doors may be any color of the rainbow, plus some that never appeared in a rainbow. The houses them-selves may also be colored, especially in the small towns and the villages. Thatched cottages—which have roofing of straw or reeds tied together—are primarily a thing of the past, except in areas popular with tourists.

A Wordy Gift from Ireland

The gift of gab, called blarney, supposedly stems from the County Cork town of Blarney. Back in the sixteenth century, the castle owner kept talking and talking, say-ing flattering things to Queen Elizabeth I but never actually surrendering the castle as he had been ordered to do. "It's all blarney!" she stormed. "He'll never do what he says." Insincere speech has been "blarney" ever since.

Timeline

Irish History		World History
The first people arrive in Ireland.	**About** **6000** B.C.	
Farming people arrive in Ireland.	**About** **4000** B.C.	
Celtic people called Gaels arrive in Ireland.	**About** **700** B.C.	2500 B.C. Egyptians build the Pyramids and Sphinx in Giza.
		563 B.C. Buddha is born in India.
St. Patrick brings Christianity to Ireland.	**About** A.D. **400**	A.D. 313 The Roman emperor Constantine recognizes Christianity.
The Vikings control Ireland.	795–1014	610 The prophet Muhammad begins preaching a new religion called Islam.
Brian Bórú's troops defeat the Vikings at the Battle of Clontarf.	1014	
		1054 The Eastern (Orthodox) and Western (Roman) Churches break apart.
		1066 William the Conqueror defeats the English in the Battle of Hastings.
Ireland comes under the control of English kings.	1171	1095 Pope Urban II proclaims the First Crusade.
		1215 King John seals the Magna Carta.
		1300s The Renaissance begins in Italy.
		1347 The Black Death sweeps through Europe.
		1453 Ottoman Turks capture Constantinople, conquering the Byzantine Empire.
		1492 Columbus arrives in North America.
Henry VIII of England is also named king of Ireland and tries to establish the Protestant Church in Ireland.	1541	1500s The Reformation leads to the birth of Protestantism.
Land in what is now Northern Ireland is given to English settlers.	1603	
Catholic King James II loses the throne of England and flees to Ireland.	1688	
Protestant King William III of Orange defeats the forces of James II and gains control of Ireland in Battle of the Boyne.	1690	
King William signs the Penal Laws taking away political rights from Catholics.	1695	
		1776 The Declaration of Independence is signed.
		1789 The French Revolution begins.

Irish History

Act of Union brings England, Scotland, Wales, and Ireland together.	1800
Parliament passes the Catholic Emancipation Act, which ends the Penal Laws and lets Irishmen become members of Parliament.	1829
Ireland suffers through the potato famine, or the Great Hunger.	1845–1851
The Irish Republican Brotherhood (IRB) is founded, with the Irish Republican Army (IRA) as its military wing.	1858
The Sinn Féin political party is founded.	1905
The IRB leads the Easter Rising.	1916
Sinn Féin wins 73 seats in Parliament but sets up an Irish legislature instead.	1918
The British Parliament passes the Government of Ireland Act, creating two Irelands.	1920
Éamon de Valera writes a new constitution for the Republic of Ireland.	1937
The Irish government breaks all ties with Great Britain and declares Ireland an independent republic.	1948
Prime Minister Sean Lemass starts a program to improve the Republic's economy.	1959
Catholics in Northern Ireland demand equal rights with Protestants, leading to decades of conflict.	1960s
The Republic of Ireland joins the European Union.	1973
Pope John Paul II visits Dublin.	1979
Companies from other countries begin operating in Ireland.	1990
IRA agrees to a cease-fire in Northern Ireland.	1994
President Bill Clinton visits Northern Ireland.	1995
The Good Friday Accord is signed with Protestants and Catholics agreeing to share power in Northern Ireland; David Trimble and John Hume receive the Nobel Peace Prize.	1998
The British government returns power to the assembly in Northern Ireland.	2000
The euro replaces the punt as the Republic of Ireland's currency.	2002

World History

1865	The American Civil War ends.
1914	World War I breaks out.
1917	The Bolshevik Revolution brings Communism to Russia.
1929	Worldwide economic depression begins.
1939	World War II begins, following the German invasion of Poland.
1945	World War II ends.
1957	The Vietnam War starts.
1969	Humans land on the moon.
1975	The Vietnam War ends.
1979	Soviet Union invades Afghanistan.
1983	Drought and famine in Africa.
1989	The Berlin Wall is torn down as Communism crumbles in Eastern Europe.
1991	Soviet Union breaks into separate states.
1992	Bill Clinton is elected U.S. president.
2000	George W. Bush is elected U.S. president.

Fast Facts

Official names: Éire and Ireland, Republic of Ireland; Northern Ireland

Capitals: Dublin, Republic of Ireland; Belfast, Northern Ireland

Official languages: Gaelic and English, Republic of Ireland; English, Northern Ireland

Dublin and the River Liffey

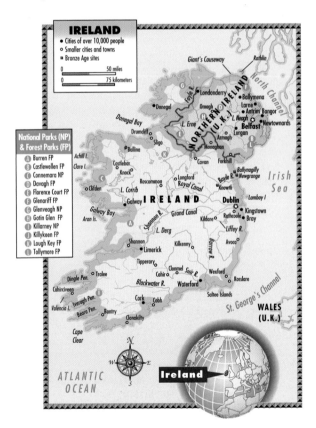

IRELAND
- Cities of over 10,000 people
- Smaller cities and towns
- Bronze Age sites

0   50 miles
0   75 kilometers

National Parks (NP) & Forest Parks (FP)
- A Burren FP
- B Castlewellen FP
- C Connemara NP
- D Davagh FP
- E Florence Court FP
- F Glenariff FP
- G Glenveagh NP
- H Gotin Glen FP
- I Killarney NP
- J Killykeen FP
- K Lough Key FP
- L Tollymore FP

Ireland's flag

Standing stone

Official religion:	None
Years of founding:	1948, Republic of Ireland; 1920, Northern Ireland
National anthem:	"The Soldier's Song," Republic of Ireland
Government:	Republic with two-house legislature, Republic of Ireland; part of Britain's constitutional monarchy with its own assembly, Northern Ireland
Chiefs of state:	President, Republic of Ireland; Queen of England, Northern Ireland
Heads of government:	Prime minister, Republic of Ireland; prime minister of United Kingdom, Northern Ireland
Area and dimensions:	32,595 square miles (84,421 sq km)
Greatest distance north to south:	302 miles (486 km)
Greatest distance east to west:	171 miles (275 km)
Latitude and longitude of geographic center:	53° North, 8° West, Republic of Ireland
Land and water borders:	North Channel to northeast, Irish Sea to east, St. George's Channel to southeast, Celtic Sea to south, North Atlantic Ocean to west
Highest elevation:	Carrauntoohill, 3,414 feet (1,041 m) above sea level, Republic of Ireland
Lowest elevation:	1.3 feet (0.4 m) below sea level at The Marsh near Downpatrick, Northern Ireland
Average temperature extremes:	35°F (2°C) on eastern coast of Northern Ireland in January; 61°F (16°C) in Belfast and Cork in July

Giant's Causeway

Etching Waterford crystal

Average precipitation extremes: 27 inches (69 cm) in the east; 60 inches (152 cm) in the southwest

National population (2000 est.): 3,797,257, Republic of Ireland; 1,663,300, Northern Ireland

Population of largest cities (2001 est.):

Greater Dublin	986,000
Cork	186,400
Limerick	82,000
Galway	59,400
Waterford	45,700
Belfast, Northern Ireland	257,000

Famous landmarks:
- ▶ *Blarney Castle*
- ▶ *The Burren*
- ▶ *Cliffs of Moher*
- ▶ *Giant's Causeway*
- ▶ *Glenveagh National Park*
- ▶ *Killarney National Park*
- ▶ *Ring of Kerry*

Industry: Service industries and manufacturing are the Republic of Ireland's largest industries. Because Ireland has so many visitors, tourism is an important service industry. Computers, software, medicines, china and linen are leading manufactured goods. In Northern Ireland, shipbuilding and aircraft building are leading industries.

Currency: On July 1, 2002, the euro will become the only legal currency in the Republic, replacing the pound, or punt. The pound will remain the currency of Northern Ireland.

Irish children

Mary Robinson

System of weights and measures: The metric system is the official system of weights and measures, but imperial measures are still used for some liquids.

Literacy: 99 percent (1997)

Common Gaelic words and phrases:

Cé mhéid? Kay vaid?	How much?/ How many?
Dia Dhuit. Dee-a gwit.	Hello, or God be with you.
Níl/Ní hea. Neel/Nee hah.	No.
Slán Agat. Slawn aguth.	Goodbye.
Táim go maith. Thawn gohmoh.	I'm fine.
Tá/Sea. Thaw/shah.	Yes.

Famous Irish:

Gerry Adams	(1948–)
Northern Ireland political leader	
Éamon de Valera	(1882–1975)
Republic of Ireland political leader	
Seamus Heaney	(1939–)
Northern Ireland poet	
John Hume	(1937–)
Northern Ireland political leader	
James Joyce	(1882–1941)
Writer	
Charles Stewart Parnell	(1846–1891)
Political leader	
Mary Robinson	(1944–)
Republic of Ireland political leader	
David Trimble	(1944–)
Northern Ireland political leader	
W. B. Yeats	(1865–1939)
Poet	

To Find Out More

Nonfiction

▶ Brady, Ciaran, ed. *The Encyclopedia of Ireland: An A-Z Guide to Its People, Places, History, and Culture.* New York: Oxford University Press, 2000.

▶ Conroy, John. *Belfast Diary: War as a Way of Life.* Boston: Beacon Press, 1995.

▶ Kent, Deborah. *Dublin.* Cities of the World. Danbury, CT: Children's Press, 1997.

▶ Levy, Patricia. *Ireland.* Cultures of the World. New York: Marshall Cavendish, 1994.

▶ McMahon, Patricia. *One Belfast Boy.* Photographs by Alan O'Connor. Boston: Houghton Mifflin, 1999.

Fiction

▶ Hunter, Mollie. *The Smartest Man in Ireland.* New York: Harcourt, 1996.

▶ Lenihan, Eddie, et al. *Stories of Old Ireland for Children.* Irish American Book Co., 1998. Available from: 6309 Monarch Park Place, Niwot, CO, 80503.

Biography

▶ Bloom, Harold, ed. *William Butler Yeats.* Bloom's Major Poets. Broomall, PA: Chelsea House Publishing, 2001.

▶ Carter, Alan. *U2: The Road to POP.* London: Faber & Faber, 1997.

▶ Edwards, Owen Dudley. *Éamon de Valera.* Washington, DC: Catholic University of America Press, 1989.

▶ Sayers, Peig. *Peig.* Syracuse, NY: Syracuse University Press, 1991.

▶ Taylor, Alice. *To School Through the Fields: An Irish Country Childhood.* New York: St. Martin's Press, 1994.

Videos

▶ *The Beauty of Ireland* (2 tapes). Covers Donegal, Dublin, Cork, and Kerry. American Home Treasures.

▶ *Irish Dancing Step by Step*. Ainm Music.

▶ *Irish Ways*. About the conflict in Northern Ireland. First Run/Icarus Films. 1989.

▶ *Legends of Ireland* (3 tapes). 1998.

▶ *One Island, Two Irelands*. Original archival material on the history of Ireland. First Run/Icarus Films. 1998.

Websites

▶ **Go Ireland**
http://www.goireland.com
This Website provides information about touring Ireland and includes maps.

▶ **Welcome to Northern Ireland**
http://interknowledge.com/
northern-ireland.
The official site for the Northern Ireland Tourist Board displays maps and offers a great deal of information about historical locations, mountains, glens, and moors.

▶ **Ireland**
http://www.irlgov.ie
At the official website of the government of Ireland, find out about administrative offices, read biographies of current leaders, and see photos of well-known locations.

▶ **The Northern Ireland Executive**
http://www.northernireland.gov.uk
The official Northern Ireland government site provides current information on the administration, legislation, and issues.

▶ **Ireland Now**
http://www.ireland-now.com/
around/index.html
This site features information about Ireland including geography, education, symbols, and education with pictures and maps.

Embassies and Consulates

▶ **Republic of Ireland Embassy**
2234 Massachusetts Ave., NW
Washington, DC 20008
(202) 462-3939

▶ **Consulate General Ireland House**
345 Park Avenue—17th Floor
New York, NY 10154-0037
(212) 319-2555

▶ **Northern Ireland Tourist Board**
551 Fifth Avenue, Suite 701
New York, NY 10176
(212) 922-0101 or (800) 326-0036

Index

Page numbers in *italics* indicate illustrations.

Meet the Author

JEAN F. BLASHFIELD delights in learning lots of fascinating, though not always important, things about places and the people who live in them. She says that when writing a book for young people, she's often as challenged by what to leave *out* of the book as by what to put in. She has long been particularly intrigued by Ireland, because of her heritage and love of things Celtic.

She has been a traveler since she went on a college choir tour of Europe and made up her mind that she would go back. After developing *The Young People's Science Encyclopedia* for Children's Press, she kept that promise to herself and returned to London to live. It was in London where she began to write books for young people. That city became her headquarters for three years of travel throughout the British Isles and the Continent. It was then that she traveled to Ireland for the first time, before the Troubles and before the wonderful burgeoning growth.

Since then, she has returned to Europe often (but not often enough! she says) while writing nearly one hundred books, most of them for young people. She likes best to write

about interesting places, but she loves history and science, too. In fact, one of her big advantages as a writer is that she becomes fascinated by just about every subject she investigates. She has created an encyclopedia of aviation and space, written popular books on murderers and on house plants, and had a lot of fun creating an early book on the things women have done, called *Hellraisers, Heroines, and Holy Women.*

She was the founder of the *Dungeons & Dragons* book department at TSR, Inc., and became avidly interested in medieval history. Nowadays she has trouble keeping the fantasy out of her medieval world, but she thinks she stuck to the facts in her coverage of medieval Ireland in this book.

Jean Blashfield was born in Madison, Wisconsin, and has lived in many other places. She graduated from the University of Michigan and worked for publishers in Chicago and Washington, D.C. But she returned to the Lake Geneva area in southern Wisconsin when she married Wallace Black (a publisher, writer, and pilot) and began to raise a family. She has two children (one is a medievalist), three cats, and two computers in her Victorian home in Delavan. In addition to researching via her computers, she produces whole books on the computer—scanning pictures, creating layouts, and even developing the index. She has become an avid Internet surfer and is working on her own website, but she'll never give up her trips to the library, and to other countries.

Photo Credits